First World War
and Army of Occupation
War Diary
France, Belgium and Germany

32 DIVISION
14 Infantry Brigade,
Brigade Machine Gun Company
1 February 1916 - 28 February 1918

WO95/2394/4

The Naval & Military Press Ltd
www.nmarchive.com
Published in association with The National Archives

Published by

The Naval & Military Press Ltd

Unit 10 Ridgewood Industrial Park,

Uckfield, East Sussex,

TN22 5QE England

Tel: +44 (0) 1825 749494

www.naval-military-press.com

www.nmarchive.com

This diary has been reprinted in facsimile from the original. Any imperfections are inevitably reproduced and the quality may fall short of modern type and cartographic standards.

© **Crown Copyright**
Images reproduced by permission of The National Archives, London, England, 2015.

Contents

Document type	Place/Title	Date From	Date To
Heading	WO95/2394 Feb 16-Feb 18 14 Inf Bde MGC.		
Heading	32nd Division 14th Infy Bde 14th Machine Gun Coy. Feb 1916-Feb 1918		
Heading	14th Brigade. 32nd Division. 14th Brigade Machine Gun Company February 1916		
War Diary	Beaucourt	01/02/1916	12/02/1916
War Diary	Beaucourt Albert	13/02/1916	13/02/1916
War Diary	Albert	14/02/1916	29/02/1916
Heading	14th Brigade. 32nd Division. 14th Brigade Machine Gun Company March 1916		
War Diary	Albert	01/03/1916	31/03/1916
Heading	14th Brigade. 32nd Division. 14th Brigade Machine Gun Company April 1916		
War Diary	Albert	01/04/1916	03/04/1916
War Diary	Albert Bouzincourt	04/04/1916	04/04/1916
War Diary	Bouzincourt	05/04/1916	11/04/1916
War Diary	Bouzincourt Warloy	12/04/1916	12/04/1916
War Diary	Warloy	13/04/1916	23/04/1916
War Diary	Contay	24/04/1916	30/04/1916
Heading	14th Brigade. 32nd Division. 14th Brigade Machine Gun Company May 1916		
War Diary	Contay	01/05/1916	04/05/1916
War Diary	Contay Warloy	05/05/1916	05/05/1916
War Diary	Warloy Bouzincourt	06/05/1916	06/05/1916
War Diary	Bouzincourt	07/05/1916	17/05/1916
War Diary	Bouzincourt Senlis	18/05/1916	18/05/1916
War Diary	Senlis	19/05/1916	29/05/1916
War Diary	Senlis Contay	29/05/1916	29/05/1916
War Diary	Contay	30/05/1916	31/05/1916
Heading	14th Brigade. 32nd Division 14th Brigade Machine Gun Company. June 1916		
War Diary	Contay	01/06/1916	11/06/1916
War Diary	Contay Warloy.	12/06/1916	12/06/1916
War Diary	Warloy Bouzincourt	13/06/1916	13/06/1916
War Diary	Bouzincourt	14/06/1916	23/06/1916
War Diary	Bouzincourt Warloy	24/06/1916	24/06/1916
War Diary	Warloy	25/06/1916	27/06/1916
War Diary	Bouzincourt Senlis Road	28/06/1916	28/06/1916
War Diary	Senlis	29/06/1916	30/06/1916
Heading	14th Bde. 32nd Div. 14th Machine Gun Company. July 1916		
War Diary	On Active Operations Trenches East Of Authville	01/07/1916	03/07/1916
War Diary	Senlis	04/07/1916	04/07/1916
War Diary	Forceville	05/07/1916	06/07/1916
War Diary	Forceville Bouzincourt.	07/07/1916	07/07/1916
War Diary	Bouzincourt	08/07/1916	09/07/1916
War Diary	In Active Operations Trenches West of Ovillers	09/07/1916	12/07/1916
War Diary	Bouzincourt	13/07/1916	14/07/1916
War Diary	Bouzincourt Warloy	15/07/1916	15/07/1916
War Diary	Warloy Beauval	16/07/1916	16/07/1916

War Diary	Beauval Le Souich	17/07/1916	17/07/1916
War Diary	Le Souich	18/07/1916	18/07/1916
War Diary	Le Souich Sibiville	19/07/1916	19/07/1916
War Diary	Sibiville Marquay	20/07/1916	20/07/1916
War Diary	Marquay St Nicholas Cauchy-A-La Tour	21/07/1916	21/07/1916
War Diary	St. Nicholas Cauchy-A-La Tour	22/07/1916	26/07/1916
War Diary	Ruitz	26/07/1916	28/07/1916
War Diary	Ruitz Annezin	29/07/1916	29/07/1916
War Diary	Annezin	30/07/1916	31/07/1916
Heading	14th Brigade. 32nd Division. 14th Brigade Machine Gun Company August 1916		
War Diary	Annezin	01/08/1916	03/08/1916
War Diary	Annezin Beuvry	04/08/1916	04/08/1916
War Diary	Beuvry	05/08/1916	05/08/1916
War Diary	Beuvry Le Preol	06/08/1916	06/08/1916
War Diary	Le Preol	07/08/1916	31/08/1916
Heading	14th Brigade. 32nd Division. 14th Brigade Machine Gun Company September 1916		
War Diary	Le Preol	01/09/1916	07/09/1916
War Diary	Le Preol Bethune	07/09/1916	07/09/1916
War Diary	Bethune	08/09/1916	15/09/1916
War Diary	Bethune Beuvry	15/09/1916	15/09/1916
War Diary	Beuvry	16/09/1916	30/09/1916
Heading	14th Brigade. 32nd Division. 14th Brigade Machine Gun Company October 1916		
War Diary	Beuvry	01/10/1916	02/10/1916
War Diary	Beuvry Bethune	03/10/1916	03/10/1916
War Diary	Bethune	04/10/1916	09/10/1916
War Diary	Bethune Busnes	10/10/1916	10/10/1916
War Diary	Busnes	11/10/1916	14/10/1916
War Diary	Busnes Raimbert	15/10/1916	15/10/1916
War Diary	Raimbert Rocourt St Laurent	16/10/1916	16/10/1916
War Diary	Rocourt St Laurent Rebreuve	17/10/1916	17/10/1916
War Diary	Rebreuve Beauval	18/10/1916	18/10/1916
War Diary	Beauval	19/10/1916	21/10/1916
War Diary	Warloy	22/10/1916	22/10/1916
War Diary	Warloy Brickfields Bouzincourt Albert Road	23/10/1916	23/10/1916
War Diary	Brickfields Bouzincourt Albert Road	24/10/1916	26/10/1916
War Diary	Harponville	27/10/1916	31/10/1916
Operation(al) Order(s)	14th Machine Gun Coy. Operation Order No. 9	22/10/1916	22/10/1916
Heading	C.C. 14th Machine Gun Coy.		
Heading	14th Brigade. 32nd Division. 14th Brigade Machine Gun Company November 1916		
War Diary	Harponville	01/11/1916	12/11/1916
War Diary	Harponville V.12c 7.8	13/11/1916	13/11/1916
War Diary	V.12c 7.8	14/11/1916	14/11/1916
War Diary	V.12c 7.8 Mailley Maillet	15/11/1916	15/11/1916
War Diary	Mailley Maillet	16/11/1916	24/11/1916
War Diary	Mailly Maillet Authieule	25/11/1916	25/11/1916
War Diary	Authieule Pernois Halloy	26/11/1916	26/11/1916
War Diary	Pernois Halloy	27/11/1916	30/11/1916
Heading	14th Brigade 32nd Division. 14th Brigade Machine Gun Company December 1916		
War Diary	Halloy	01/12/1916	05/01/1917
War Diary	Halloy Beaval	06/01/1917	06/01/1917
War Diary	Beauval Courcelles	07/01/1917	07/01/1917

War Diary	Courcelles	08/01/1917	20/01/1917
War Diary	Courcelles Mailly Maillet	21/01/1917	21/01/1917
War Diary	Mailly Maillet	22/01/1917	17/02/1917
War Diary	Mailly Maillet Harponville	18/02/1917	18/02/1917
War Diary	Harponville Warloy	19/02/1917	19/02/1917
War Diary	Warloy	20/02/1917	20/02/1917
War Diary	Warloy-Villers Bocage	21/02/1917	21/02/1917
War Diary	Villers Bocage-St Acheul	22/02/1917	22/02/1917
War Diary	St Acheul Thennes	23/02/1917	23/02/1917
War Diary	Thennes-Beaucort	24/02/1917	24/02/1917
War Diary	Beaucort Bois-Longues (E25b)	25/02/1917	25/02/1917
War Diary	Bois-Longues K22d 2.9	26/02/1917	26/02/1917
War Diary	K22d 2.9.	27/02/1917	28/02/1917
Miscellaneous	A Form. Messages And Signals.		
War Diary	K22d 2.9. K22b 35.40.	01/03/1917	01/03/1917
War Diary	K22b 35.40	02/03/1917	08/03/1917
War Diary	K22b 35.40 Beaucourt	09/03/1917	09/03/1917
War Diary	Beaucourt	10/03/1917	14/03/1917
War Diary	E3a 9.5	15/03/1917	17/03/1917
War Diary	Liancourt	18/03/1917	18/03/1917
War Diary	Liancourt Nesle Mesnil St Nicaise	19/03/1917	19/03/1917
War Diary	Mesnil St Nicaise	20/03/1917	20/03/1917
War Diary	Mesnil St Nicaise Voyennes	21/03/1917	21/03/1917
War Diary	Voyennes	22/03/1917	27/03/1917
War Diary	Voyennes Beauvois	28/03/1917	28/03/1917
War Diary	Beauvois	29/03/1917	31/03/1917
War Diary	Beauvois Chateau-De Pommery	01/04/1917	01/04/1917
War Diary	Rear H.Qrs Chateau-De Pommery Forward H.Qrs. Savy	02/04/1917	06/04/1917
War Diary	Savy Foreste	07/04/1917	07/04/1917
War Diary	Foreste	08/04/1917	11/04/1917
War Diary	Forward Hd Qrs Savy. Rear Hd. Qrs Germaine	12/04/1917	13/04/1917
War Diary	Savy	14/04/1917	20/04/1917
War Diary	Savy Quivieres	21/04/1917	21/04/1917
War Diary	Quivieres	22/04/1917	14/05/1917
War Diary	Quivieres Offoy	15/05/1917	15/05/1917
War Diary	Offoy Liancourt	16/05/1917	16/05/1917
War Diary	Liancourt Warvillers	17/05/1917	17/05/1917
War Diary	Warvillers Le Quesnel	18/05/1917	18/05/1917
War Diary	Le Quesnel	19/05/1917	29/05/1917
War Diary	Le Quesnel Marcelcave	30/05/1917	30/05/1917
War Diary	Marcelcave	31/05/1917	31/05/1917
Miscellaneous	A Form. Messages And Signals.	01/07/1917	01/07/1917
War Diary	Marcelcave	01/06/1917	01/06/1917
War Diary	A21 A6.8	02/06/1917	12/06/1917
War Diary	A21 A6.8 Q8CID Eecke Area	13/06/1917	13/06/1917
War Diary	Eecke	14/06/1917	14/06/1917
War Diary	Eecke Tetegham	15/06/1917	15/06/1917
War Diary	Teteghem	16/06/1917	16/06/1917
War Diary	Teteghem & Coxyde	17/06/1917	17/06/1917
War Diary	Coxyde	18/06/1917	19/06/1917
War Diary	Nieuport	20/06/1917	26/06/1917
War Diary	Coxyde	27/06/1917	28/06/1917
War Diary	Coxyde Nieuport	29/06/1917	29/06/1917
War Diary	Nieuport	30/06/1917	05/07/1917
War Diary	Nieuport Coxyde	06/07/1917	06/07/1917

War Diary	Coxyde	07/07/1917	09/07/1917
War Diary	Coxyde & X6.A.3.8. Sheet 11.5E 1/20000	10/07/1917	10/07/1917
War Diary	X6A 3.8. Sheet 115E 1/20000	11/07/1917	11/07/1917
War Diary	X6A.3.8	12/07/1917	12/07/1917
War Diary	X.6.A.3.8. & Nieuport	13/07/1917	13/07/1917
War Diary	Nieuport	14/07/1917	19/07/1917
War Diary	Coxyde & Leffringhouck C29.C.1.1	20/07/1917	20/07/1917
War Diary	Leffringhoucke C.29.c.1.1	21/07/1917	01/08/1917
War Diary	Coxyde	02/08/1917	11/08/1917
War Diary	Rear H.Qrs Coxyde Forward H.Qrs Newport M.28 C.80.27.	12/08/1917	16/08/1917
War Diary	W22b2.8	16/08/1917	16/08/1917
War Diary	Rear. H.Q. W 22 B2.8 Forward H.Q Nieuport M.28C80.27.	17/08/1917	17/08/1917
War Diary	Camp At W.22 B2.8.	18/08/1917	26/08/1917
War Diary	Camp at W. 22 B.2.8 Australia Camp. Rear H.Q. Nieuport forward H.Q. (M.34.a.8.5.	27/08/1917	27/08/1917
War Diary	Australia Camp (Rear H.Q. Nieuport M.34a.8.5. (Forward H.Q)	28/08/1917	31/08/1917
War Diary	Coy H.Qrs. Nieuport Transport At Australia Camp	01/09/1917	02/09/1917
War Diary	Coxyde Coy H.Qrs Nieuport Transport At Australia Camp Coxyde	03/09/1917	04/09/1917
War Diary	Coy H.Qrs Nieuport Rear HQRS At Australia Camp Coxyde.	05/09/1917	08/09/1917
War Diary	Coy H.Qrs. Nieuport.	09/09/1917	09/09/1917
War Diary	Nieuport	10/09/1917	11/09/1917
War Diary	Coy H.Qrs At Nieuport	12/09/1917	12/09/1917
War Diary	Coy Hqrs Nieuport Rear Hqrs Australia Camp	13/09/1917	13/09/1917
War Diary	Australia Camp Coxyde	14/09/1917	20/09/1917
War Diary	Canada Camp Coxyde Three Kings Farm M.32D.31.	21/09/1917	21/09/1917
War Diary	Three Kings Farm M.32.D.31	22/09/1917	27/09/1917
War Diary	Three Kings Farm	28/09/1917	28/09/1917
War Diary	Three Kings Farm M32D.2.1 & M.29.c.2060.	29/09/1917	29/09/1917
War Diary	M.32.D.31	30/09/1917	30/09/1917
War Diary	Hd Qrs M.29.C.2060	01/10/1917	06/10/1917
War Diary	Hd Qrs At M.29.C.20.60. & Australia Camp W.22.B.28.	07/10/1917	07/10/1917
War Diary	Australia Camp Coxyde (W.22.B.22	08/10/1917	08/10/1917
War Diary	Coudekerque Branche H.11.A.90.00	09/10/1917	25/10/1917
War Diary	Eringhem T.22.D.8.7	26/10/1917	26/10/1917
War Diary	Ledringhem Arneke. Area C.27.C.9.8	27/10/1917	27/10/1917
War Diary	Ledringham C.27.C.9.8.	28/10/1917	29/10/1917
War Diary	Ledringhem	30/10/1917	31/10/1917
War Diary	Hd Qrs C27.C.9.8	01/11/1917	10/11/1917
War Diary	Oudezeele	11/11/1917	11/11/1917
War Diary	Hd Qrs. F.27.C.	12/11/1917	23/11/1917
War Diary	Hd Qrs F.27.C. Transport H 6A.5.8 B27A. 65 Transport	24/11/1917	24/11/1917
War Diary	Hd Qrs B27A.65. Transport H.6A.5.8	25/10/1917	25/10/1917
War Diary	Hd Qrs. B27A.6.5. Transport B.30.D.1.2	26/11/1917	30/11/1917
War Diary	Hd Qrs At D.4.C.80.80.	01/12/1917	10/12/1917
War Diary	Hd Qrs. at Transport At H3B 4.3	11/12/1917	17/12/1917
War Diary	Hd Qrs Canal Bank Transport At H.3.B.4.3	18/12/1917	23/12/1917
War Diary	Hd Qrs. C.11.D. 15.35 Transport H.3.B.4.3	24/12/1917	28/12/1917
War Diary	Hd Qrs C.11.D.15.35	29/12/1917	31/12/1917
Miscellaneous	14th Company Machine Gun Corps.		

War Diary	Coy Hd Qrs Bertham	01/01/1918	03/01/1918
War Diary	Coy Hd Qrs	04/01/1918	04/01/1918
War Diary	Coy Hd Qrs Bertham	05/01/1918	21/01/1918
War Diary	Coy Hd Qrs B19.d.33.	22/01/1918	29/01/1918
War Diary	Coy Hd Qrs Ambrose Camp. B.10.D	30/01/1918	31/01/1918
War Diary	Hd. Qrs V.21.C.2.1. Transport A.11.B.5.5.	08/02/1918	09/02/1918
War Diary	Hd Qrs A.H.B. 55. V.21.C.3.1	10/02/1918	10/02/1918
War Diary	Hd Qrs Dekort Camp Transport A.5.C.50.20	11/02/1918	14/02/1918
War Diary	Hd Qrs B.3.C.20.70. Transport A.5.C.50.20.	01/02/1918	01/02/1918
War Diary	Hd Qrs U.8.D.40.30. Transport A.11.b.5.5	02/02/1918	07/02/1918
War Diary	Hd Qrs Dekort Camp Transport A.5.C.50.20.	15/02/1918	20/02/1918
War Diary	Hd. Qrs. U.Q.A 2060 Transport A.11.B.5.5	21/02/1918	21/02/1918
War Diary	Hd Qrs U.9.A.2060 Transport	22/02/1918	22/02/1918
War Diary	Hd Qrs U.9.A. 2060 Transport A 11. B 5.5	23/02/1918	27/02/1918
War Diary	Hd Qrs U.9.A.2060	28/02/1918	28/02/1918

WO 95/2394

Feb' 16 — Feb' 18

14 Inf Bde   M G C.

32ND DIVISION
14TH INFY BDE

14TH MACHINE GUN COY.

FEB 1916 - FEB 1918

14th Brigade.

32nd Division.

14th BRIGADE MACHINE GUN COMPANY

FEBRUARY 1916

Army Form C. 2118.

WAR DIARY
or
INTELLIGENCE SUMMARY.

14th M.G.C. (1st GS MGC)

(Erase heading not required.)

Hour, Date, Place	Summary of Events and Information		Remarks and references to Appendices
1st February Beaumont	In billets training		
2nd February Beaumont	Do	Do	
3rd February Beaumont	Do	Do	
4th February Beaumont	Do	Do	
5th February Beaumont	Do	Do	
6th February Beaumont	Do	Do	
7th February Beaumont	Do	Do	
8th February Beaumont	Do	Do	
9th February Beaumont	Do	Do	
10th February Beaumont	Do	Do	

Army Form C. 2118.

WAR DIARY
or
INTELLIGENCE SUMMARY.
(Erase heading not required.)

Instructions regarding War Diaries and Intelligence Summaries are contained in F.S. Regs., Part II. and the Staff Manual respectively. Title pages will be prepared in manuscript.

Hour, Date, Place	Summary of Events and Information	Remarks and references to Appendices
11th February Beaucourt	In billets training.	
12th February Beaucourt	Do	{ Coy changed name from 95th Bde M.G. Coy to 14th Bde M.G. Coy }
13th February Beaucourt Albert	Coy left Beaucourt at 1-15pm & marched to Albert arriving 6pm. Went to billets. Officers made reconnaissance of trenches at Aveluy. (Weather Good.) No.266. Pte. J. Bosworth Base 13.2.16 (Time expires 1.3.16)	Do
14th February Albert	Coy went into trenches to the East of Aveluy Sectors F1 & F2. 3 sections in trenches & 1 sect in reserve. Considerable enemy shell fire.	
15th February Albert	In trenches. Weather bad.	
16th February Albert	Do	

Army Form C. 2118.

WAR DIARY
or
INTELLIGENCE SUMMARY.

(Erase heading not required.)

Instructions regarding War Diaries and Intelligence Summaries are contained in F. S. Regs., Part II. and the Staff Manual respectively. Title pages will be prepared in manuscript.

Hour, Date, Place	Summary of Events and Information	Remarks and references to Appendices
17th February. Albert.	In trenches. No 4764 Pte W. Webb to Base 17.2.16 (Same colours 23.2.16.)	
18th February. Albert.	In trenches. Section relief took place.	
19th February. Albert.	In trenches. Weather fair.	
20th February. Albert.	Do. Hd Qr dugouts Ft. heavily shelled with Howitzers.	
21st February. Albert.	In trenches. Indirect fire was commenced at the position of gun on left of Bridgehead defences (East of Ancre)	
22nd February. Albert.	In trenches. Section relief took place. Heavy shelling by enemy at night.	

(9 26 6) W5257—975 100,000 1/12 H W V 79/3298

Army Form C. 2118

WAR DIARY
or
INTELLIGENCE SUMMARY.
(Erase heading not required.)

Instructions regarding War Diaries and Intelligence Summaries are contained in F.S. Regs., Part II. and the Staff Manual respectively. Title pages will be prepared in manuscript.

Hour, Date, Place	Summary of Events and Information	Remarks and references to Appendices
23rd February. Albert.	In trenches. (Weather cold.)	
24th February. Albert.	Do (snow)	
25th February. Albert.	Do (heavy snowfall extremely cold)	
26th February. Albert.	Do (cold) Section reliefs took place.	
27th February. Albert.	In trenches. (weather fairer)	
28th February. Albert.	Do	
29th February. Albert.	Do Enemy shelled heavily from 6-0 pm to 7-30 pm.	

14th Brigade.

32nd Division.

14th BRIGADE MACHINE GUN COMPANY

MARCH 1 9 1 6:

WAR DIARY

or

INTELLIGENCE SUMMARY

of 14th Brigade Machine Gun Coy.

Army Form C. 2118

(Erase heading not required.)

Place	Date	Hour	Summary of Events and Information	Remarks and references to Appendices
ALBERT.	1.3.16		In trenches. Weather fair. Nothing to report	
ALBERT.	2.3.16		In trenches. (Weather fair.) Company took over new billets at Rue Becourt ALBERT SOUTH. Guns distributed as follows E.1 two guns E.2 two guns E.3 three guns F.1 four guns F.2 three guns. Relief completed in E. sector at 3pm. Enemy inactive.	
ALBERT.	3.3.16		In trenches (Weather wet) Enemy moderately active. Relief took place. Have teams in F.1.F.2 were relieved by the 15th M.M. Gun Battery.	
ALBERT.	4.3.16		In trenches (Weather wet & cold) Nothing to report.	
ALBERT.	5.3.16		In trenches. (Weather fair) Nothing to report.	

Army Form C. 2118

WAR DIARY or 147 Brigade Machine Gun Company

INTELLIGENCE SUMMARY

(Erase heading not required.)

Place	Date	Hour	Summary of Events and Information	Remarks and references to Appendices
ALBERT.	6.3.16		In trenches. (Weather Fair.) BRAY ST position heavily shelled, Section relief took place. "D" Section vacated WANNING ST & relieved "C" Section in CONISTON ST Section F.2. One team of "C" Section relieved the 147th Bde M.G. Coy in emplacement in CHECKERBENT ST Section G.1. "A" Section relieved the 147th Bde M.G. Coy in positions as follows TRENCH 144/ TOBERMORY AVE/ DAVAAR AVE/ SOUTH BARRIER.	
ALBERT.	7.3.16		In trenches. "D" Section took over gun in CONISTON ST Section F.2. Enemy shelled continuously round about CAMPBELL AVE, during the afternoon. Enemy knocked in part of Bridgehead appeared to be searching left of wood with Whizz Bangs at BRIDGEHEAD gun position. A red light followed by two green ones were sent up by the enemy on LA BOISSELLE front at 9.45 p.m.	
ALBERT.	8.3.16		In trenches. (Weather fine & cold.) Own artillery bombarded GERMAN front line opposite G.1 Section at 3.30 p.m. Enemy replied by shelling AUTHVILLE, BLACKHORSE RD & AVELUY WOOD.	

WAR DIARY
of 14th Brigade Machine Gun Company
INTELLIGENCE SUMMARY

Army Form C. 2118

(Erase heading not required.)

Place	Date	Hour	Summary of Events and Information	Remarks and references to Appendices
ALBERT	9.3.16		In trenches. Weather fine. Throughout the whole day enemy's artillery was active shelling AUTHUILLE WOOD & right of F.2 subsector. At eleven p.m. enemy commenced a heavy bombardment, at eleven ten p.m. enemy shell fire was concentrated on the night of G.1 & left of F.2 at this time our artillery retaliated & bombardment became intense. Bombardment ceased at 12 p.m. Slight damage done to our trenches & few casualties.	
ALBERT	10.3.16		In trenches (Weather fine) Usual shelling throughout the day. A large number of green & red lights were sent up to the left of LA-BOISSELLE during the night by the enemy.	
ALBERT	11.3.16		In trenches. (Weather fine) Both sides moderately quiet during day. At 6 p.m. our 18 pounders fired on enemy machine gun X14/A 95/50. Fire had little effect as gun continued firing during the night. Coloured lights were sent up by the enemy from "Y" east of LA BOISSELLE.	

Army Form C. 2118

WAR DIARY
of 14th Brigade Machine Gun Company
INTELLIGENCE SUMMARY

(Erase heading not required.)

Instructions regarding War Diaries and Intelligence Summaries are contained in F. S. Regs., Part II. and the Staff Manual respectively. Title Pages will be prepared in manuscript.

Place	Date	Hour	Summary of Events and Information	Remarks and references to Appendices
ALBERT	12.3.16		Both sides showed little activity during day & night. In trenches. (Weather fine.) (Relief) The 6th NORTHUMBERLAND FUS. relieved the 16th LANCASHIRE FUSILIERS.	
ALBERT	13.3.16		In trenches. (Weather fine.) Enemy artillery active during day & night.	
ALBERT.	14.3.16		In trenches. Enemy quiet during day & night around G sector. At ten p.m. two aeroplanes passed over out lines in sector G supposed to be GERMAN machines. Considerable bombing activity in E.3 sector during the night. An aeroplane flew over out lines in E.3 sector at 8.30 p.m. flying towards POZIERES.	
ALBERT	15.3.16		In trenches. Enemy shelled gun position in sector E.3 between 6 p.m. 7 p.m. The 2nd MANCHESTERS relieved the 1st DORSETS.	

1875 Wt. W593/826 1,000,000 4/15 J.B.C. & A. A.D.S.S./Forms/C. 2118.

Army Form C. 2118

WAR DIARY 14th Brigade. Machine Gun Company
or
INTELLIGENCE SUMMARY

(Erase heading not required.)

Instructions regarding War Diaries and Intelligence Summaries are contained in F. S. Regs., Part II. and the Staff Manual respectively. Title Pages will be prepared in manuscript.

Place	Date	Hour	Summary of Events and Information	Remarks and references to Appendices
ALBERT	16.3.16		In trenches. (Weather fine) 500 rounds were fired from OVILLERS POST at front X 8 B 60/75 between 8 p.m. & 12 p.m. from BRIDGE HEAD 400 rounds were fired. Three enemy machine guns replied to our fire instead of usual one. At 9-15 p.m. our billets were vacated by Transport owing to enemy shelling the vicinity of RUE BECOURT. The 96th Bde M.G. Coy relieved "A" section in G.1. Sector. "A" Section withdrew to Hd. Qr. billets ALBERT.	
ALBERT	17.3.16		In trenches. A.B.C. Sections & Transport left billets Rue Becourt at 11 A.M. & returned at 1 p.m. during this period enemy shelled ALBERT several shells landing very near by billets. At 7.30 p.m. Transport left billets owing to enemy shelling. One charger badly wounded by shell fire.	

Army Form C. 2118

WAR DIARY 14th Brigade Machine Gun Company
INTELLIGENCE SUMMARY
(Erase heading not required.)

Place	Date	Hour	Summary of Events and Information	Remarks and references to Appendices
ALBERT	18.		In trenches. (Weather fine). British & German aeroplanes very active during the day. No encounters occured. (Relief) 2/Lieut R.W. Burton with two teams of "B" Section relieved 2/Lieut G.R.H. Bailey & two teams " " " in trenches E.3. After relief 2/Lieut Bailey & teams withdrew to Hd. Qr. Billets ALBERT.	
ALBERT	19.3.16		In trenches. Enemy inactive during day. During the night sentries at OVILLERS POST & BRIDGEHEAD reported previous lights (apparently signals) in direction of AVELUY WOOD & on the Rd running over the hill WEST of ALBERT.	
ALBERT	20.3.16		In trenches. British aeroplanes active during day. Enemy shelled E. side of ALBERT with several 77 M.M. & 5.9" shells at 3.30 P.M. causing few casualties.	

WAR DIARY
of 14th K/Brigade Machine Gun Company
INTELLIGENCE SUMMARY

(Erase heading not required.)

Place	Date	Hour	Summary of Events and Information	Remarks and references to Appendices
ALBERT.	21.3.16		In trenches. "A" section relieved "D" section in district F1. & one team of "C" " " 1 team of "C" section attached to "B" section. Relieved teams withdrew to Hd. Qr. Millets Rue. Becourt Albert. Enemy sent several heavy shells into Albert at 3.30 p.m.	
ALBERT.	22.3.16		In trenches. (Weather fair) Enemy shelled ALBERT at 3.30 p.m with several heavy shells. Situation normal.	
ALBERT.	23.3.16		In trenches (Weather Wet & Cold) Enemy shelled ALBERT at 2-35 P.M. Two teams of "B" section took over gun positions in USNA REDOUBT vacated command of ? Lieut R.W. BURTON.	
ALBERT.	24.3.16		In trenches (Snowfall) Situation normal.	

WAR DIARY
of 14th Brigade Machine Gun Company.
INTELLIGENCE SUMMARY

(Erase heading not required.)

Instructions regarding War Diaries and Intelligence Summaries are contained in F.S. Regs., Part II. and the Staff Manual respectively. Title Pages will be prepared in manuscript.

Place	Date	Hour	Summary of Events and Information	Remarks and references to Appendices
ALBERT	25.3.16		In trenches. (Weather cold) GERMAN aeroplane was observed flying over out trenches at 8 a.m. but was driven back by our anti-aircraft guns.	
ALBERT	26.3.16		In trenches. (Weather mild) Both sides very quiet during the day. Three teams of "C" Section under Lieut F.G. STOTT took up positions at BRIDGEHEAD. under instructions from O.C. Coy. Hd Qr details "D" Section & portion of Transport in ALBERT stood to arms at midnight.	
ALBERT	27.3.16		In trenches. (Weather fine) At 12.27 a.m. ENGLISH exploded a mine opposite LA BOISSELLE & made a raid on "Y" sap. A few casualties were sustained. Both sides moderately quiet during the day. Relief took place "C" Section took out gun at BRIDGEHEAD DEFENCES. "A" Section took over gun in RYCROFT ST (127 TRENCH) "C" Section withdrew to Hd. Qr. billets ALBERT. The following draft arrived N° 7490 P.te F.L. AULTON. N°10325 P.te J. ATHERTON. N°26817 P.te B. FRYME. N°13641 P.te W. DAMEN. N° 3553 P.te J. ATHERTON.	

WAR DIARY
or 14 1/2 Brigade Machine Gun Company
INTELLIGENCE SUMMARY

(Erase heading not required.)

Instructions regarding War Diaries and Intelligence Summaries are contained in F. S. Regs., Part II. and the Staff Manual respectively. Title Pages will be prepared in manuscript.

Place	Date	Hour	Summary of Events and Information	Remarks and references to Appendices
ALBERT.	28.3.16		In trenches. (Weather fair) Situation normal.	
ALBERT.	29.3.16		In trenches. (Weather fair) Situation normal.	
ALBERT.	30.3.16		In trenches. (Weather fair) Situation normal.	
ALBERT.	31.3.16		In trenches. (Weather fine & mild) GERMAN & BRITISH aeroplanes very active during the day. Situation normal.	

14th Brigade.

32nd Division.

14th BRIGADE MACHINE GUN COMPANY

APRIL 1916

Army Form C. 2118

WAR DIARY
of 14th Brigade Machine Gun Coy.
INTELLIGENCE SUMMARY
(Erase heading not required.)

Instructions regarding War Diaries and Intelligence Summaries are contained in F. S. Regs., Part II. and the Staff Manual respectively. Title Pages will be prepared in manuscript.

Place	Date	Hour	Summary of Events and Information	Remarks and references to Appendices
ALBERT.	1.4.16		In trenches. Weather fine. British & German aeroplanes active during day.	
ALBERT.	2.4.16		In trenches. Weather fine. Situation Normal.	
ALBERT.	3.4.16		In trenches. Weather fine. Situation Normal.	
ALBERT. Bouzincourt.	4.4.16		Head Qrs & Transport removed to billets Bouzincourt at 4.30 p.m. Billets very poor. Sections took over positions in Sector G. (Authuille)	
BOUZINCOURT	5.4.16		In trenches. Weather fine. Situation normal.	
BOUZINCOURT	6.4.16		In trenches. Weather fine. The following draft arrived from M.G. Base as follows	

1875. Wt. W593/826 1,000,000 4/15 J.B.C. & A. A.D.S.S./Forms/C. 2118.

WAR DIARY
INTELLIGENCE SUMMARY

14th Brigade Machine Gun Company

(Erase heading not required.)

Army Form C. 2118

Place	Date	Hour	Summary of Events and Information	Remarks and references to Appendices
			April 6th continued.	
			No 15484 Private. WELSH. J.	
			" 15231 L/Corporal. LEONARD. P.	
			" 15236 Private. ALTY. T.A.	
			" 15485 Do WARE. W.	
			" 15339 Do GIBBONS. W.	
			At 9 p.m. a heavy bombardment commenced in the vicinity of G.2 Sector and ceased at 10-15 p.m.	J.J.
BOUZINCOURT.	7.4.16		In trenches. Weather fine. Situation normal.	J.J.
BOUZINCOURT.	8.4.16		In trenches. Weather fine. Situation normal.	J.J.
BOUZINCOURT.	9.4.16		In trenches. Weather fine. Situation normal.	J.J.
BOUZINCOURT.	10.4.16		In trenches. Weather fine. Situation normal.	J.J.

Army Form C. 2118

WAR DIARY

of 14 Brigade Machine Gun Company

INTELLIGENCE SUMMARY

(Erase heading not required.)

Place	Date	Hour	Summary of Events and Information	Remarks and references to Appendices
Bouzincourt.	11.4.16		In trenches. Weather Wet. Lieut G.A. Bentinck relieved Lieut C.M. Singer at BRIDGEHEAD DEFENCES.	[sig]
Bouzincourt.	12.4.16		Weather Wet. The 97th Bde M.G. Coy relieved Company in AUTHUILLE and THIEPVAL Sectors. After relief Hd. Qrs, C.D sections withdrew to rest billets WARLOY. A.B sections went in reserve in AVELUY to the Brigade in the line.	[sig]
Warloy.	13.4.16		Weather fine. Distribution of Company as follows A.B sections with gun limbers & watercart in AVELUY under the command of Lieut G.R.H. Bailey. Three teams for A.B sections, Officers chargers & two full S.A.A. limbers in Bouzincourt. Hd. Qrs, C.D sections & remainder of Transport at WARLOY.	[sig]
Warloy.	14.4.16		A.B sections at BRIDGEHEAD DEFENCES AVELUY.in reserve to the Brigade in the line C.D sections in billets WARLOY training.	[sig]

WAR DIARY

of of 114th Brigade Machine Gun Company

INTELLIGENCE SUMMARY

Army Form C. 2118

Place	Date	Hour	Summary of Events and Information	Remarks and references to Appendices
WARLOY	15.4.16		A & B sections at AVELUY in reserve to Brigade in the line. C & D sections in billets WARLOY Training.	[initials]
WARLOY	16.4.16		A & B sections at AVELUY in reserve to Brigade in the line. C & D sections attended Church Parade WARLOY.	[initials]
WARLOY	17.4.16		A & B sections at AVELUY in reserve to Brigade in the line. C & D sections in billets WARLOY training. 2/Lieut G.R.H. BAILEY joined company at WARLOY. 2/Lieut R.W. BURTON took over command of A & B sections in AVELUY.	[initials]
WARLOY	18.4.16		Weather Wet. A & B sections at AVELUY in reserve to Bde in the line. C & D sections in billets WARLOY training.	[initials]
WARLOY	19.4.16			[initials]
WARLOY	20.4.16		Section relief took place. C & D sections under the command of Lieut F.G. STOTT relieved A & B sections in AVELUY. After relief A & B sections under the command of 2/Lieut R.W. BURTON withdrew to rest billets WARLOY vacated by C & D sections.	[initials]

Army Form C. 2118

WAR DIARY
of 14th Brigade Machine Gun Company
INTELLIGENCE SUMMARY
(Erase heading not required.)

Place	Date	Hour	Summary of Events and Information	Remarks and references to Appendices
WARLOY	21.4.16		C & D sections at AVELUY in reserve to Brigade in the line. A & B sections in billets WARLOY training.	
WARLOY	22.4.16		Do	
WARLOY	23.4.16		C & D sections relieved by 96th Bde. M.G. Coy. Relief complete 2.p.m. After relief C.D. sections under LIEUT F. G. STOTT marched to rest billets CONTAY via ALBERT, MILLENCOURT, & HENENCOURT. A & B sections, portion of transport, old GR details handed at Company billets 2.15.p.m. & marched to starting point road junction U.23 d 9/6 2.30 p.m. & then proceeded via VADENCOURT to rest billets CONTAY. Portion of transport stationed at BOUZINCOURT joined company at CONTAY with gun etc of O'D section. Sixteen New VICKERS guns & twelve cases of spare parts received from 32nd DIVISION ORDNANCE to replace sixteen MAXIMS & spare part boxes.	

Army Form C. 2118

WAR DIARY
or 14th Brigade Machine Gun Company
INTELLIGENCE SUMMARY
(Erase heading not required.)

Instructions regarding War Diaries and Intelligence Summaries are contained in F.S. Regs., Part II. and the Staff Manual respectively. Title Pages will be prepared in manuscript.

Place	Date	Hour	Summary of Events and Information	Remarks and references to Appendices
CONTAY	24.4.16		Weather fine. In billets CONTAY. A. B. C. & D sections took over new VICKERS guns from Fed. Station. Sixteen MAXIMS returned to 32ND DIVISION ORDNANCE.	
CONTAY	25.4.16		In billets CONTAY training.	
CONTAY	26.4.16		Do	
CONTAY	27.4.16		Whole Company bar billet guard on Divisional tactical scheme from 8.30 A.M. to 2.30 P.M.	
CONTAY	28.4.16		In billets CONTAY training.	
CONTAY	29.4.16		In billets CONTAY training. Company attended Flammenwerfer demonstration at U22B6/1 1,200 yards N.E. of VADENCOURT.	

Army Form C. 2118

WAR DIARY
of 141th Brigade Machine Gun Company
INTELLIGENCE SUMMARY

(Erase heading not required.)

Instructions regarding War Diaries and Intelligence Summaries are contained in F. S. Regs., Part II. and the Staff Manual respectively. Title Pages will be prepared in manuscript.

Place	Date	Hour	Summary of Events and Information	Remarks and references to Appendices
CONTAY	30.4.16		In billets CONTAY training Company billets & Transport lines inspected by Brig. General COMPTON at 11.a.m. Church Parade 11.30 a.m. Seven officers & twenty O.R. attended Lecture Theatre SENLIS on Machine Gun Tactics 3 p.m.	W.

14th Brigade.

32nd Division.

<u>14th BRIGADE MACHINE GUN COMPANY</u>

<u>M A Y   1 9 1 6</u>

Army Form C. 2118.

WAR DIARY

INTELLIGENCE SUMMARY

of 4 Bde Machine Gun Company

(Erase heading not required.)

Vol 4

Place	Date	Hour	Summary of Events and Information	Remarks and references to Appendices
CONTAY	1.5.16		Whole company less guard on Divisional tactical scheme 8 A.M. to 3-45 P.M.	
CONTAY	2.5.16		In Billets training.	
CONTAY	3.5.16		In Billets training.	
CONTAY	4.5.16		Whole company less Billet guard on Divisional tactical scheme 8 A.M. to 3-45 P.M.	
CONTAY WARLOY	5.5.16		A & B sections marched via WARLOY — HENENCOURT — MILLENCOURT — ALBERT to AVELUY and relieved two sections of the 97 Bde Machine Gun Coy there. Remainder of Company (less A & B sections) marched to WARLOY & took over billets vacated by 96 Bde Machine Gun Coy.	

Instructions regarding War Diaries and Intelligence Summaries are contained in F.S. Regs., Part II. and the Staff Manual respectively. Title Pages will be prepared in manuscript.

Army Form C. 2118

WAR DIARY
or
INTELLIGENCE SUMMARY
(Erase heading not required.)

of "B" 5th Machine Gun Company

Place	Date	Hour	Summary of Events and Information	Remarks and references to Appendices
WARLOY / BOUZINCOURT	6.5.16		Company relieved the 97th Bde Machine Gun Coy in the line as follows. "A" Section took over Wood Post group. "B" " " " Authuille " "C" " " " Authuille Wood group. "D" " " " Bridgehead " Company Hd. Qrs & Ad. Qr. details at Bouzincourt. Situation in trenches normal.	
BOUZINCOURT	7.5.16		A. B. C & D. Sections in trenches. From 10 a.m. till 6 p.m. a [illegible] duel took place between our batteries and enemy artillery. At 11 p.m. this marked a climax and the enemy began an intense bombardment which spread from Wood Post to the left towards THIEPVAL. Support and communication trenches were shelled heavily. Enemy raised our line [illegible] opposite THIEPVAL	

Army Form C. 2118

WAR DIARY
or
INTELLIGENCE SUMMARY
(*Erase heading not required.*)

Instructions regarding War Diaries and Intelligence Summaries are contained in F.S. Regs., Part II. and the Staff Manual respectively. Title Pages will be prepared in manuscript.

Place	Date	Hour	Summary of Events and Information	Remarks and references to Appendices
BOUZINCOURT	8.5.16		A, B, C & D Sections in trenches. Situation Normal.	
BOUZINCOURT	9.5.16		Do	
BOUZINCOURT	10.5.16		Do. One O.R. wounded by shrapnel 10.a.m.	
BOUZINCOURT	11.5.16		Sections in trenches. Enemy bombarded our trenches from 1-45 a.m. till 2-15 a.m. Situation quiet during remaining 21 ¾ hours.	
BOUZINCOURT	12.5.16		Sections in trenches. Situation Normal.	
BOUZINCOURT	13.5.16		Do	

Army Form C. 2118

WAR DIARY
OF
86th Machine Gun Company
INTELLIGENCE SUMMARY

(Erase heading not required.)

Instructions regarding War Diaries and Intelligence Summaries are contained in F.S. Regs., Part II. and the Staff Manual respectively. Title Pages will be prepared in manuscript.

Place	Date	Hour	Summary of Events and Information	Remarks and references to Appendices
Bouzincourt	14.5.16		Sections in trenches. At 11 p.m. the enemy opened fire on our lines with rapid rifle and machine gun fire followed by a short but heavy bombardment with shrapnel and large calibre mortars. Bombardment lasted ten minutes, much damage to trenches and few casualties.	
Bouzincourt	15.5.16		Sections in trenches. Enemy bombarded trenches heavily on left of THIEPVAL WOOD from 12-30 A.M. to 1-30 A.M.	
Bouzincourt	16.5.16		Sections in trenches. Situation normal.	
Bouzincourt	17.5.16			

WAR DIARY
INTELLIGENCE SUMMARY of 14th Bde Machine Gun Coy.

Army Form C. 2118

(Erase heading not required.)

Place	Date	Hour	Summary of Events and Information	Remarks and references to Appendices
BOUZINCOURT SENLIS	18.5.16		Company was relieved in the line by the 9th Bde. Machine Gun Coy. After relief A & B sections withdrew to rest billets SENLIS via ALBERT & BOUZINCOURT arriving at 7.a.m. C & D sections withdrew to AVELUY & were attached to the 9th Bde. M.G. Coy as garrison of AVELUY. Company H.Q Rs. and Transport took over billets & Transport lines in SENLIS. Lieut A.L. HYSLOP joined company from Machine Gun Corps Base Depot CAMIERS.	
SENLIS	19.5.16		A & B sections in Billets training. C & D " in garrison of AVELUY.	
SENLIS	20.5.16		Do Do	
SENLIS	21.5.16		One O.R. evacuated to BASE (expiration of service June 24th 1916)	

Army Form C. 2118

WAR DIARY
of
INTELLIGENCE SUMMARY 1st Bde Machine Gun Company

(Erase heading not required.)

Instructions regarding War Diaries and Intelligence Summaries are contained in F. S. Regs., Part II. and the Staff Manual respectively. Title Pages will be prepared in manuscript.

Place	Date	Hour	Summary of Events and Information	Remarks and references to Appendices
Senlis	23.5.16		A & B Sections in Billets training. C & D " in garrison of Aveluy. Eight O.R. reinforcements joined Company from Base Garniers.	
Senlis	24.5.16		At 3p.m. A & B Sections under the command of Lieut C.M. Singer left for billets Senlis and marched to Aveluy via Northumberland Avenue & Pioneer Road and relieved there C & D Sections. After relief C & D Sections under the command of Lieut F.G. Stott marched to Hd. Qrs. Senlis via Pioneer Road & Northumberland Avenue arriving at 7-30p.m. and took over billets vacated by A & B Sections.	
Senlis	25.5.16		A & B Sections in garrison of Aveluy. C & D " in Billets training.	

WAR DIARY
INTELLIGENCE SUMMARY 14th Bde Machine Gun Coy
(Erase heading not required.)

Army Form C. 2118

Instructions regarding War Diaries and Intelligence Summaries are contained in F.S. Regs., Part II. and the Staff Manual respectively. Title Pages will be prepared in manuscript.

Place	Date	Hour	Summary of Events and Information	Remarks and references to Appendices
SENLIS	26.5.16		A & B Sections in garrison of AVELUY. C & D " " " " Five O.R. reinforcements joined Company from M.G. Corps Base Depot CAMIÉRS.	
SENLIS	27.5.16		A & B Sections in garrison of AVELUY. C & D " " " " Billets training.	
SENLIS	28.5.16		Do	
SENLIS	29.5.16		A & B Sections relieved in AVELUY by half Company of 97 Bde Machine Gun Company. Relief complete 1 h.m. At 1-15 p.m. A & B Sections under the command of Lieut C. M. SINGER left AVELUY & marched via PIONEER RD & NORTHUMBERLAND AVENUE—BOUZINCOURT to SENLIS arriving 3 h.m. At 6-15 h.m. whole Company & transport	

Army Form C. 2118

WAR DIARY
or
INTELLIGENCE SUMMARY 14 Bde Machine Gun Coy.
(Erase heading not required.)

Instructions regarding War Diaries and Intelligence Summaries are contained in F.S. Regs., Part II. and the Staff Manual respectively. Title Pages will be prepared in manuscript.

Place	Date	Hour	Summary of Events and Information	Remarks and references to Appendices
SENLIS CONTAY	29.5.16	Contd	in column of route left SENLIS and marched via WARLOY to CONTAY arriving at 8.a.m. Company took over billets vacated by 96 D Bde M.G. Coy.	
CONTAY	30.5.16		Whole Company in Billets training.	
CONTAY	31.5.16		Company paraded at 8-30 a.m. in marching order & was inspected by C.O. preparatory to G.O.C.'s inspection. At 10.10 a.m. G.O.C. inspected company in Marching order, with Transport.	

14th Brigade.
32nd Division.

14th BRIGADE MACHINE GUN COMPANY

JUNE 1916::

14th Brigade.
32nd Division.

14th BRIGADE MACHINE GUN COMPANY

JUNE 1916::

WAR DIARY of INTELLIGENCE SUMMARY

Army Form C. 2118

XXXII 2nd Bde. Machine Gun Coy Vol 3

Place	Date	Hour	Summary of Events and Information	Remarks and references to Appendices
CONTAY	1.6.16	4 a.m to 12-30 p.m	Company took part in Tactical Exercise with the 14th Infantry Bde in conjunction with the III Corps on the BEHENCOURT BRIZIEUX training area.	
CONTAY	2.6.16		Company in Billets training.	
CONTAY	3.6.16		Company on Route march 8 a.m to 12.30 p.m.	
CONTAY	4.6.16	11.30 a.m.	Company excepting R.C.'s attended Brigade Church Parade.	
CONTAY	5.6.16		Company in Billets training.	
CONTAY	6.6.16	11 a.m.	Transport inspected by Divisional Commander. (Weather very Wet)	
CONTAY	7.6.16		Company on tactical training 9-30 a.m. to 12.30 p.m.	
CONTAY	8.6.16	4 a.m to 12.30	Company on tactical scheme with 14 Infantry Bde on the BEHENCOURT BRIZIEUX training ground. (Weather very Wet)	

WAR DIARY
OF
INTELLIGENCE SUMMARY

Army Form C. 2118

14 Divl. Machine Gun Coy

Place	Date	Hour	Summary of Events and Information	Remarks and references to Appendices
CONTAY	9.6.16	9 a.m. to 12-30 p.m. 1.45 p.m. 7 p.m.	Company in Billets training. 14 Infantry Bde Assault at Arms took place.	
CONTAY	10.6.16		Company in Billets training.	
CONTAY	11.6.16		All denominations excepting R.C.s attended Church of England parade at 11 a.m. R.C.s attended Holy Mass 9 a.m.	
CONTAY WARLOY	12.6.16	10 a.m.	C & D sections left Company billets & marched to Aveluy & relieved there half Coy of 96 Bde M.G. Coy. Relief complete 1-45 p.m. A & B sections on Divisional Tactical Exercise on the BEHENCOURT - BAIZIEUX training area from 7.15 a.m. to 12-30 p.m. After Tactical Exercise A & B Sections marched to Billets WARLOY vacated by the 97 D. Bde M.G. Coy. Company Hd Qrs moved to WARLOY.	

Army Form C. 2118

WAR DIARY
of
28th Machine Gun Coy
INTELLIGENCE SUMMARY
(Erase heading not required.)

Place	Date	Hour	Summary of Events and Information	Remarks and references to Appendices
WARLOY BOUZINCOURT	13.6.16		Company Head. Qrs. moved to Bouzincourt. Company relieved the 96 B. Bde. M.G. Coy in the line as follows, gun positions taken over in THIEPVAL SECTOR as follows:- WHITCHURCH ST. GOMMEL ST. CATERPILLAR WOOD. THIEPVAL AVENUE. } "D" Section WOOD POST CHEQUERBENT ST. ROCK ST. BURY AVENUE } "C" Section KEEPS IN AUTHUILLE WOOD. MAJOR GENERALS EMPLACEMENT } "B" Section BRIDGEHEAD & VALLEY EMPLACEMENT } "A" Section	Summary

Army Form C. 2118

WAR DIARY
of 4th Bn. Machine Gun Coy.
INTELLIGENCE SUMMARY

(Erase heading not required.)

Instructions regarding War Diaries and Intelligence Summaries are contained in F. S. Regs., Part II. and the Staff Manual respectively. Title Pages will be prepared in manuscript.

Place	Date	Hour	Summary of Events and Information	Remarks and references to Appendices
BOUZINCOURT	4.6.16		Company in trenches. (Situation Normal)	M. Myatt jun
BOUZINCOURT	5.6.16		DAYLIGHT SAVING. Time advanced sixty minutes at (11pm became 12 midnight.)	
BOUZINCOURT	6.6.16		Company in trenches (Situation Normal) On O.R. Reinforcement joined Coy from Base.	
BOUZINCOURT	6.6.16		Company in trenches (Situation Normal) 16. O.Rs Reserve Machine Gunners att. to Coy.	W Thuey Mur
BOUZINCOURT	7.6.16		Company in trenches (Situation Normal) Much aerial activity on both sides.	
BOUZINCOURT	8.6.16		Company in trenches. Much aerial activity on both sides during the whole day. Enemy shelled trenches behind Woodpost with 5.9 shells from 10 a.m. to 12 p.m. Enemy bombarded THIEPVAL SECTOR with Minenwerfers from 8 p.m. to 9 p.m.	

Army Form C. 2118

WAR DIARY of
INTELLIGENCE SUMMARY 14 Coy Machine Gun Coy

(Erase heading not required.)

Instructions regarding War Diaries and Intelligence Summaries are contained in F. S. Regs., Part II. and the Staff Manual respectively. Title Pages will be prepared in manuscript.

Place	Date	Hour	Summary of Events and Information	Remarks and references to Appendices
BOUZINCOURT	19.6.16		Company in trenches. Situation normal.	Payn
BOUZINCOURT	20.6.16		Do. 1. O.R. wounded Gonards Emplacement	Forster
BOUZINCOURT	21.6.16		Company in trenches. Situation normal.	
BOUZINCOURT	22.6.16		Do.	Forster
BOUZINCOURT	23.6.16		Do.	
BOUZINCOURT WARLOY	24.6.16		Company relieved in the line by the 25th, 96th & 9th Coy MGC Machine Gun Coys. After relief Coy marched to billets WARLOY (Very heavy storm)	

Army Form C. 2118

WAR DIARY
or
INTELLIGENCE SUMMARY 14th Bde Machine Gun Coy

(Erase heading not required.)

Instructions regarding War Diaries and Intelligence Summaries are contained in F. S. Regs., Part II. and the Staff Manual respectively. Title Pages will be prepared in manuscript.

Place	Date	Hour	Summary of Events and Information	Remarks and references to Appendices
WARLOY	25.6.16		R.C.'s Church parade 9-45 a.m. C of E " " not held.	
WARLOY	26.6.16		Whole day spent in preparing guns & equipment for active operations.	
WARLOY	27.6.16		At 9-45 p.m. Company paraded outside by billets. At 10 p.m. Coy marching in rear of the 19th Lan. Fus., left Warloy & marched to assembly trenches AUTHUILLE. Transport moved to Brigade Transport Lines Bouzincourt Senlis ROAD. (Beaucourt Dist.)	
BOUZINCOURT SENLIS ROAD	28.6.16		Company returned from assembly trenches AUTHUILLE WOOD to billets Senlis arriving at 6-15 a.m. 29th inst. Operation postponed 48 hours.	

1875. Wt. W593/826 1,000,000 4/15 T R.C. & A. A.D.S.S./Forms/C. 2118.

WAR DIARY
or
INTELLIGENCE SUMMARY 1/4 Batt. Cheshire ~~Coy~~

Army Form C. 2118

(Erase heading not required.)

Place	Date	Hour	Summary of Events and Information	Remarks and references to Appendices
Senlis	29.6.16		Company in Billets Senlis.	
Senlis	30.6.16		At 9 p.m. Coy paraded in fighting order at transport lines Bouzincourt Senlis Road. At 9.10 p.m. Hd. Qrs., A & B Sections marched in rear of the 19th Lan. Fus. to Blackhorse Bridge Shelters, clearing cross roads W.13.a.5.9 at 9-45 p.m. and forming point W.10.c.1.5 at R.O. midnight. C & D Sections Sergt Ewen & 12 Gunners followed 13-2 H.L.I. to Crucifix Corner clearing Eastern Ravine of Bouzincourt at 10-20 p.m. Sections were attached with units 1/4 Inf Bde as follows - A 7 B Section with 1st Dorsets - C Sect. in reserve - D Sect. with 2nd Manchesters. Coy went in G Black Horse dug outs	

R. Hurlyhur
1/4 Bde M.G. Coy

14th Bde.
32nd Div.

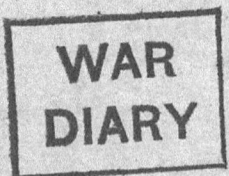

14th MACHINE GUN COMPANY.

JULY 1916

WAR DIARY or INTELLIGENCE SUMMARY

Army Form C. 2118

of 4 Bn. Machine Gun Coy

Place	Date	Hour	Summary of Events and Information	Remarks and references to Appendices

IN ACTIVE OPERATIONS

TRENCHES EAST OF AUTHUILLE

1.7.16 — General attack on Enemy positions in which Bgy was taking part was ordered for this day.

At Zero time Coy was distributed as follows:

- 8 Guns with 1st DORSET REGT.
- 4 " " 2nd MANCHESTER REGT.

(Guns were to advance with these Battalions and were to take up positions in the allotted objectives when these were reached. Brigade objective was German 2nd line from R.34a 6/9 to R.21.c.2/7)

4 Guns in Reserve.

When main attack was held up by Machine Gun fire two guns were sent to our front line trench with orders to search fort and reduce hostile Machine Gun Post. These guns got into action. Two guns were sent up with and to support the attack of 19th Lan. Fus.
Both these guns moving across the open from DUMBARTON TRACK reached our front line trench.

Sig MGO37 OS£ 20

KoHW

1875 Wt. W593/826 1,000,000 4/15 J.B.C. & A. A.D.S.S./Forms/C. 2118.

Army Form C. 2118

WAR DIARY
or
INTELLIGENCE SUMMARY 1/4 2 Bn. Machine Gun Coy

(Erase heading not required.)

Place	Date	Hour	Summary of Events and Information	Remarks and references to Appendices
—	1.7.16	—	**contd.** One gun was completely destroyed by shell fire. At this time orders were received that our attack would continue from our front line trench. Five guns moved up Rook St. to our front line trench. Orders were received that the attack was postponed and all these guns then withdrew to the barricade in ROOK ST. Early in the afternoon the MANCHESTERS attacked LEIPZIG SALIENT. Four guns supported this attack — two went forward with leading Coy and got into fourteen in the German trenches two remaining in reserve in our own front line. These guns remained with the 2ND MANCHESTERS and were not relieved by the 96 Bde M.G. Coy according to our orders.	
IN "ACTIVE OPERATIONS" TRENCHES EAST OF AUTHUILLE	2.7.16	—	On the morning of the 2nd the 2nd 7 guns were assembled in shelter trenches AUTHUILLE WOOD. At this period disposition were as follows 4 guns with 2ND MANCHESTER REGT. 7 " " " 7 " in SHELTER TRENCHES above RESERVE.	

Army Form C. 2118

WAR DIARY
or
INTELLIGENCE SUMMARY 14 Bde Machine Gun Coy
(Erase heading not required.)

Instructions regarding War Diaries and Intelligence Summaries are contained in F.S. Regs, Part II. and the Staff Manual respectively. Title Pages will be prepared in manuscript.

Place	Date	Hour	Summary of Events and Information	Remarks and references to Appendices
—	2.7.16	—	contd. During afternoon 4 guns in reserve relieved guns with 2ND MANCHESTERS in LEIPZIG SALIENT. This relief was carried out that front to relief of 2ND MANCHESTERS by 15 D H.L.I. Four additional guns moved with 15D H.L.I. to our original front line with orders to cover attack by that Battalion. During the afternoon carried out by 15D H.L.I. on the morning of the 3rd two of the guns in LEIPZIG SALIENT got into action in good targets, and guns caught Germans retiring across the open; the other came into action later on a communication trench up which the enemy were trying to reinforce. A number of Germans were put out of action and the trench made untenable.	8/ MM FRANCE 870 S. Gains [?]
IN ACTIVE OPERATIONS IN TRENCHES EAST OF AUTHUILLE.	3.7.16		During afternoon 4th QRs and remaining guns = 7 moved to Reserve in AUTHUILLE DEFENCES. The Company was relieved by the 7R Bde M.G. Coy on the night of the 3/4th July and withdrew to SENLIS. Throughout operations the whole completement of ammunition (less that carried through casualties was maintained with guns.	

WAR DIARY
of
INTELLIGENCE SUMMARY

Army Form C. 2118

34th Div. Machine Gun Coy.

Place	Date	Hour	Summary of Events and Information	Remarks and references to Appendices
—	3.7.16	contd	Total casualties as follows:- 1st wk. 1 officer Wounded. 2 O.R. Killed 26 O.R. Wounded.	
SENLIS	4.7.16		Company in Billets.	
FORCEVILLE	5.7.16		Company moved to FORCEVILLE arriving 8.15 p.m.	
FORCEVILLE	6.7.16		Company in Billets.	
FORCEVILLE BOUZINCOURT	7.7.16		Coy moved to BOUZINCOURT (Corps Reserve). During night enemy shelled BOUZINCOURT with about ten 5-9 shells doing little damage. Heavy bombardment around OVILLERS all day.	

Army Form C. 2118

WAR DIARY
or of
INTELLIGENCE SUMMARY 14 Bde Machine Gun Coy
(Erase heading not required.)

Place	Date	Hour	Summary of Events and Information	Remarks and references to Appendices
BOUZINCOURT	8.7.16	-	Company in Corps Reserve.	
"ACTIVE OPERATIONS IN TRENCHES WEST OF OVILLIERS"	9.7.16	-	On the morning of the 9 inst Coy relieved the 36th Bde M.G. Coy. Guns were distributed as follows:— 4 in OVILLIERS. 3 " RYCROFT. ST 4 " W.180 shooting indirect on enemy trenches north of OVILLIERS. 4 " Reserve. At 9 p.m on this day 2 guns from reserve went forward to support the 13 D.H.L.I. Three guns got into action at (approx) points x 8.c.8.3 and about 1 a.m were able to fire on enemy working in a communication trench. The guns shooting indirect have fired 5,000 rounds at their target during this day.	nil

Army Form C. 2118

WAR DIARY
or of
INTELLIGENCE SUMMARY 14 Bn. Machine Gun Coy
(Erase heading not required.)

Instructions regarding War Diaries and Intelligence Summaries are contained in F.S. Regs., Part II. and the Staff Manual respectively. Title Pages will be prepared in manuscript.

Place	Date	Hour	Summary of Events and Information	Remarks and references to Appendices
IN "ACTIVE OPERATIONS" TRENCHES WEST OF OVILLERS.	10.7.16	—	At 2-15 a.m. on the 10th inst the guns north of Ovillers R.S. fired on an enemy bombing party. One gun team located a German sniper and shot him. At 5 p.m. the remaining two guns in reserve went forward to support the attack of the 8th Bn. Two other guns were mounted in the Captured German trench just south of point 13. They did not come into action.	J.R.
IN "ACTIVE OPERATIONS" TRENCHES WEST OF OVILLERS.	11.7.16	—	At 3 a.m. on the 11th inst a gun in position at X 8c 2.9 got into action on a party of Germans moving in the open towards the trench recently taken by the Inniskilling Fus. The enemy disappeared. The gun also engaged a German machine gun which was playing the one of our bombing parties, temporarily silencing it. The guns doing indirect fire were heavily shelled for three hours. At midday on the 12th inst the Coy was relieved by	
IN "ACTIVE OPERATIONS" TRENCHES WEST OF OVILLERS.	12.7.16			

Army Form C. 2118

WAR DIARY
or
INTELLIGENCE SUMMARY
(Erase heading not required.)

of 14 Bde Machine Gun Coy

Place	Date	Hour	Summary of Events and Information	Remarks and references to Appendices
—	12.7.16	—	Contd / the 96 Bde M.G. Coy. Casualties during period were 1 Officer killed, 1 O.R. " , 7 O.R. Wounded	J.H.
Bouzincourt	13.7.16		Company in Billets.	J.H.
Bouzincourt	14.7.16		Company in Billets. Lieut Owen Bentley joined Coy from Base.	J.H.

1875 Wt. W593/826 1,000,000 4/15 J.B.C. & A. A.D.S.S./Forms/C. 2118.

WAR DIARY
INTELLIGENCE SUMMARY 14th Bde Machine Gun Coy

Army Form C. 2118

(Erase heading not required.)

Place	Date	Hour	Summary of Events and Information	Remarks and references to Appendices
BOUZINCOURT WARLOY.	15.7.16		At 2-50 p.m. Coy moved via Q route to Billets WARLOY arriving 6 p.m. Company attached 96th Infantry Bde.	K.M.
WARLOY. BEAUVAL.	16.7.16		At 11 A.M. Coy left WARLOY & marched via VARRENS - LEALVILLERS - ARQUEVES - RAINQUEVAL - BEAUQUENSE - RAINNEVAL to BEAUVAL arriving 6-30 p.m.	R.M. R? Rd. map BEGINS!! 100,000 K.M.
BEAUVAL LE SOUICH	17.7.16		Company marched from BEAUVAL via DUELLENS - HTE VISSE to LESOUICH arrived 7 k.m.	K.M.
LE SOUICH	18.7.16		Company resting in Billets.	K.M.

Army Form C. 2118

WAR DIARY
or
INTELLIGENCE SUMMARY 14th Div. Machine Gun Coy
(Erase heading not required.)

Instructions regarding War Diaries and Intelligence Summaries are contained in F.S. Regs., Part II. and the Staff Manual respectively. Title Pages will be prepared in manuscript.

Place	Date	Hour	Summary of Events and Information	Remarks and references to Appendices
LE SOUICH SIBIVILLE	19.7.16		At 8 A.M. Coy moved with 14th Infantry Bde to the area MONTS-EN-TERNOIS - MONCHEUX - SIBIVILLE. By the following route:- [own roads ½ mile north] LENSH - ARBRES ARBRE - LA COUTURE - REBREUVE - MONVAL - SIBIVILLE. Company arrived in Billets SIBIVILLE 11.25 A.M.	By M.R.
SIBIVILLE MARQUAY	20.7.16		At 8 A.M. Coy moved with the 14th Infantry to the area MONCHY-BRETON - ORLENCOURT - OSTREVILLE - MARQUAY by Route:- TERNAS - LIGNY - ST FLOCHEL to MARQUAY. Company arrived in Billets MARQUAY 11 A.M.	
MARQUAY ST NICHOLAS CROUCHY-A-LA TOUR	21-7.16		At 6-30 A.M. Coy moved with 14th Infantry Bde to the area RAIMBERT - CAUCHY-A-LA-TOUR FLORINGHEM. Company arrived in Billets ST NICHOLAS - CROUCHY-A-LA-TOUR at 11-55 A.M.	

1875 Wt. W593/826 1,000,000 4/15 J.B.C. & A. A.D.S.S./Forms/C.2118.

Army Form C. 2118

WAR DIARY
or
INTELLIGENCE SUMMARY

(Erase heading not required.)

Instructions regarding War Diaries and Intelligence Summaries are contained in F. S. Regs., Part II. and the Staff Manual respectively. Title Pages will be prepared in manuscript.

Place	Date	Hour	Summary of Events and Information	Remarks and references to Appendices
ST. NICHOLAS CAUCHY-A-LA-TOUR	22.7.16		Company in Billets.	
ST. NICHOLAS CAUCHY-A-LA-TOUR	23.7.16		Company in Billets.	
ST. NICHOLAS CAUCHY-A-LA-TOUR	24.7.16		At 9-30A.M. Half Coy. moved forward to HOUCHIN. joined 17D NORTHUMBERLAND FUS. at HOUCHIN at 11 A.M. and became att to 40th Division.	Ref. Sheet I 16A 6/8 36 B. 1/40,000
ST. NICHOLAS CAUCHY-A-LA-TOUR	25.7.16		Half Coy in Billets.	
ST. NICHOLAS CAUCHY-A-LA-TOUR	26.7.16		Half Company moved to the area RUITZ- HOUCHIN MARLES-LES-MINES PLACE-A-BRUAY. Company arrived in Billets RUITZ 1-15 P.M.	
RUITZ	27.7.16		Half Company inspected by G.O.C. 14th Infantry Bde 9-15 a.m.	

Army Form C. 2118

WAR DIARY
or
INTELLIGENCE SUMMARY 14th Bde Machine Gun Coy
(Erase heading not required.)

Place	Date	Hour	Summary of Events and Information	Remarks and references to Appendices
RUITZ	28.7.16		14 Infantry Bde inspected by Army Commander at 3 p.m.	
RUITZ ANNEZIN	29.7.16		Company moved to ANNEZIN. Route via E.10.D.4.3. E.9.B.5.7. having starting point E.16.a.2.8. at 9.42 a.m. Company arrived in billets ANNEZIN 11.30 a.m.	Ref sheets 36 R.1. 36 N.W.
ANNEZIN	30.7.16		Company in billets training	
ANNEZIN	31.7.16		Company in billets training	

J.A. Decrospigny Maj
O.C. 14 Bde M.G. Coy
31/7/16

14th Brigade.

32nd Division.

14th BRIGADE MACHINE GUN COMPANY

AUGUST 1 9 1 6

Army Form C. 2118

WAR DIARY
of
INTELLIGENCE SUMMARY 14 Brigade Machine Gun Coy

(Erase heading not required.)

Instructions regarding War Diaries and Intelligence Summaries are contained in F.S. Regs., Part II. and the Staff Manual respectively. Title Pages will be prepared in manuscript.

Place	Date	Hour	Summary of Events and Information	Remarks and references to Appendices
ANNEZIN	1.8.16		Half Coy. in billets Annezin training. Map Sh 36 N.E. 1/1/20,000	Appx
			" " in garrison of Loos (att to 2nd Division)	
ANNEZIN	2.8.16		Do	
ANNEZIN	3.8.16		Half Coy in billets Annezin training. "2nd M.G. Coy." garrison of Loos relieved by 96th M.G. Coy. Relief compl.Feb 11-15 P.M. Half Coy marched via PETIT SAINS & NŒUX LES MINES arriving BEUVRY 3am next day	Appx
ANNEZIN BEUVRY	4.8.16		Half Company at Annezin moved to billets BEUVRY arriving 10-45 a.m. and joined there half company which had been attached to the 40 Division	Appx

2449 Wt. W14957/M90 750,000 1/16 J.B.C. & A. Forms/C.2118/12.

Army Form C. 2118:

WAR DIARY
of
INTELLIGENCE SUMMARY of 4 Machine Gun Company

(Erase heading not required.)

Instructions regarding War Diaries and Intelligence Summaries are contained in F. S. Regs., Part II. and the Staff Manual respectively. Title Pages will be prepared in manuscript.

Place	Date	Hour	Summary of Events and Information	Remarks and references to Appendices
BEUVRY.	5.8.16		Company less 1 Section relieved the 142 Machine Gun Company on the line (Givenchy Sector) as follows.	
			3 guns on Canal Bank by "A" Section	
			3 guns in Brick Stacks	
			3 guns " Grafton Street by "B" Section	
			1 gun " Marylebone Rd } by "C" Section	
			1 " " Tower R & R St. }	
			2 guns " Kingsway	
			Reserve Beuvry "D" Section	
BEUVRY	6.8.16		Company less 1 Section in trenches (Givenchy Sector)	
LE PREOL			Head Quarters and Reserve Section with transport moved to billets L.E. Preol arriving 5.30 p.m.	

Army Form C. 2118.

WAR DIARY
of
INTELLIGENCE SUMMARY
(Erase heading not required.)

Instructions regarding War Diaries and Intelligence Summaries are contained in F. S. Regs., Part II. and the Staff Manual respectively. Title Pages will be prepared in manuscript.

2nd Shropshire Light Infantry

Place	Date	Hour	Summary of Events and Information	Remarks and references to Appendices
LE PREOL	7.8.16		Company two Reserve Section in trenches (Quinchy Sector) Situation Normal.	
LE PREOL	8.8.16		do	
LE PREOL	9.8.16		do	
LE PREOL	10.8.16		do	

Army Form C. 2118.

WAR DIARY
or
INTELLIGENCE SUMMARY (↑ 2ⁿᵈ Machine Gun Coy)

(Erase heading not required.)

Instructions regarding War Diaries and Intelligence Summaries are contained in F. S. Regs., Part II. and the Staff Manual respectively. Title Pages will be prepared in manuscript.

Place	Date	Hour	Summary of Events and Information	Remarks and references to Appendices
Le Preol	11.8.16		Company less (1 Section in Reserve) in trenches (CUINCHY SECTOR) Situation Normal.	[initials]
	11.8.16		Lieut F. A. HELLABY proceeded to join 109ᵗʰ M.G. Coy. to take over command as temporary Captain.	[initials]
Le Preol	12.8.16		Company less (1 Section in Reserve) in trenches CUINCHY SECTOR. Situation Normal.	[initials]

2449 Wt. W14957/M90 750,000 1/16 J.B.C. & A. Forms/C.2118/12.

Army Form C. 2118.

WAR DIARY
of
INTELLIGENCE SUMMARY of 2 Machine Gun Company
(Erase heading not required.)

Instructions regarding War Diaries and Intelligence Summaries are contained in F. S. Regs., Part II. and the Staff Manual respectively. Title Pages will be prepared in manuscript.

Place	Date	Hour	Summary of Events and Information	Remarks and references to Appendices
Le Preol	13.8.16		Reference map 36 NE/20,000 7.35" W 1/40,000 Company Relief took place as follows:— "D" Section in Reserve took over positions 8 to 11 inclusive. "A" Section took over positions 8 to 11 inclusive. "B" Section " " 1 to 4 " "C" Section withdrawn to billets Le Preol. Situation Normal.	
Le Preol	14.8.16		Coy. (less 1 section in Reserve) in trenches Cuinchy Sector. Situation Normal.	

Army Form C. 2118.

WAR DIARY
of 3. Machine Gun Coy.
INTELLIGENCE SUMMARY 14 Machine Gun Coy.

(Erase heading not required.)

Instructions regarding War Diaries and Intelligence Summaries are contained in F. S. Regs., Part II. and the Staff Manual respectively. Title Pages will be prepared in manuscript.

Place	Date	Hour	Summary of Events and Information	Remarks and references to Appendices
Le Preol.	15.8.16		Sheets Sheet 36 N.E. & 36 N.W. 1/20,000 1/10,000 Coy (less 1 section in Reserve) in trenches Cuinchy Sector. Situation Normal.	
Le Preol.	16.8.16		Coy (less 1 section in Reserve) in trenches Cuinchy Sector. Situation Normal.	
Le Preol.	17.8.16			

Army Form C. 2118.

WAR DIARY
of
INTELLIGENCE SUMMARY [2nd Bn. Queens Own Cameronians]
(Erase heading not required.)

Place	Date	Summary of Events and Information	Remarks and references to Appendices

| LE PREOL. | 18.8.16 | [Signed] H. Mintoch 2/Lt N Ellis ADC 2/5 N.U.F./2/2 [illegible] | |

Company Relief took place as follows:—

"C" Section in Reserve took over positions 8 to 11 inclusive.

"D" Section took over positions 4 to 11 inclusive.

"A"   "   "   "   1 to 3 "

"B" Section withdrew to billets Le. Preol.

Coy (Rev. Section in Reserve) in Trenches

CUINCHY SECTOR.

Situation Normal.

| LE PREOL. | 19.8.16 | | |

WAR DIARY or INTELLIGENCE SUMMARY

Army Form C. 2118.

11th Machine Gun Company

(Erase heading not required.)

Place	Date	Hour	Summary of Events and Information	Remarks and references to Appendices
LE PREOL.	20.8.16		Sheet 36 N.E. 1/20000 36 C.N.W. 1/10.000 Coy (less 1 Section in Reserve) in trenches GUINCHY SECTOR. Situation normal.	
LE PREOL.	21.8.16		Do	
LE PREOL.	22.8.16		Do Bristol aeroplane brought down by enemy anti-aircraft gun fire 6-30 p.m. Lieut E. WIGLEY joined Coy as 2nd in Command from 2/11th L. Coy.	
LE PREOL.	23.8.16		Company Relief took place as follows :— "D" Section in Reserve took over positions 9 to 11 inclusive. "C" Section took over positions 5 to 8 inclusive.	

2449 Wt. W14957/M90 750,000 1/16 J.B.C. & A. Forms/C.2118/12.

Army Form C. 2118.

WAR DIARY
of
INTELLIGENCE SUMMARY of 13 E Machine Gun Coy.

(Erase heading not required.)

Instructions regarding War Diaries and Intelligence Summaries are contained in F. S. Regs., Part II. and the Staff Manual respectively. Title Pages will be prepared in manuscript.

Place	Date	Hour	Summary of Events and Information	Remarks and references to Appendices
LE PREOL	26.8.16		Ref Maps 36 N.E 1/20,000 36 C N.W 1/40,000 Company (Hear & Section in Reserve) in Trenches GUINCHY SECTOR. Situation Normal.	
LE PREOL	27.8.16		2nd Lieut. M. Simms joined Company from Base.	
LE PREOL	28.8.16		(By Relief.) The following reliefs took place:- "A" Section in Reserve, took over positions 9 to 11 inclusive, 1 team of "B" Section took over position No 8. "B" Section (Hears & team) took over positions 5 & 7 inclusive. "C" " " took over positions 1 to 4 inclusive. "D" " " withdrew to Billets LA PREOL. Situation normal.	

Army Form C. 2118.

WAR DIARY
or
INTELLIGENCE SUMMARY 1st Machine Gun Company

(Erase heading not required.)

Instructions regarding War Diaries and Intelligence Summaries are contained in F. S. Regs., Part II. and the Staff Manual respectively. Title Pages will be prepared in manuscript.

Place	Date	Hour	Summary of Events and Information	Remarks and references to Appendices
			General	
Le Preol.	23.8.16		"D" Section took over positions 1 to 4 inclusive. "A" " " " to billets Le Preol. Relief complete 12-15 p.m. Situation normal.	
Le Preol.	24.8.16		Coy (less 1 section in Reserve) in trenches Cuinchy Sector. Situation normal.	
Le Preol.	25.8.16			

WAR DIARY
of
INTELLIGENCE SUMMARY of the Machine Gun Company

Army Form C. 2118.

(Erase heading not required.)

Place	Date	Hour	Summary of Events and Information	Remarks and references to Appendices
LE PREOL	29.8.16		Map Sheet 36 NE & 36 N. W 1/20.000	
			Coy (less 1 Section in Reserve) in trenches Cuinchy Sector. Situation normal. 2nd Lieut D.G. Kydd [returned to join 170 M.G. Coy on secondment from us.]	
LE PREOL	30.8.16		" Weather very hot.	
LE PREOL	31.8.16		Coy (less 1 Section in Reserve) in trenches Cuinchy Sector. Situation normal.	

[signatures]
Major O.C. 14th M.G. Coy
H.H. 31st

14th Brigade.

32nd Division.

14th BRIGADE MACHINE GUN COMPANY

SEPTEMBER 1 9 1 6

14th Brigade.

32nd Division.

14th BRIGADE MACHINE GUN COMPANY

SEPTEMBER 1 9 1 6

Army Form C. 2118.

WAR DIARY
of
INTELLIGENCE SUMMARY 114th Machine Gun Company
(Erase heading not required.)

Instructions regarding War Diaries and Intelligence Summaries are contained in F.S. Regs., Part II. and the Staff Manual respectively. Title Pages will be prepared in manuscript.

Place	Date	Hour	Summary of Events and Information	Remarks and references to Appendices
Le Preol	1.9.16		Company (less 1 section in reserve) in trenches Cuinchy Sector. Situation normal.	
Le Preol	2.9.16		Company relief took place as follows:— "D" section (less 1 gun) took over position 9 to 11 inclusive, 1 team of "D" section attached to "B" section took over N.9 position. "A" section (less 1 gun) took over positions 5 to 7 inclusive. "B" section took over positions 1 to 4 inclusive. "C" section on relief returned to billets L.E. Preol. Relief complete 11.45 p.m. Situation normal.	

2449 Wt. W14957/Mg0 750,000 1/16 J.B.C. & A. Forms/C.2118/12.

WAR DIARY

INTELLIGENCE SUMMARY 4th S. Midland Machine Gun Coy

(Erase heading not required.)

Army Form C. 2118.

Instructions regarding War Diaries and Intelligence Summaries are contained in F. S. Regs., Part II. and the Staff Manual respectively. Title Pages will be prepared in manuscript.

Place	Date	Hour	Summary of Events and Information	Remarks and references to Appendices
LE PREOL	3.9.16		Map Ref 1/20000 26. N.31.a.9.d. 26.N.31.c.0.5.3. Company (also 1 section in reserve) in trenches GUINCHY SECTOR. Situation normal.	TDC
LE PREOL	4.9.16		＂	TDC
LE PREOL	5.9.16		＂	TDC
LE PREOL	6.9.16		＂	TDC
LE PREOL	7.9.16		Company relieved on the line (GUINCHY SECTOR) by 97th Dn Machine Gun Coy. Relief completed 3 p.m. After relief Headquarters transport and	TDC

Army Form C. 2118.

WAR DIARY
of
INTELLIGENCE SUMMARY of [illegible] E [illegible] Company

(Erase heading not required.)

Instructions regarding War Diaries and Intelligence Summaries are contained in F. S. Regs., Part II. and the Staff Manual respectively. Title Pages will be prepared in manuscript.

Place	Date	Hour	Summary of Events and Information	Remarks and references to Appendices
LAPREOL BETHUNE	7.9.16	6am	Sections marched to new billets BETHUNE. (Ref ref E 17 A.8.3)	[illeg]
BETHUNE	8.9.16		Company in billets training	[illeg]
BETHUNE	9.9.16		½	[illeg]
BETHUNE	10.9.16		Company attended C. of E. parade at 9.30 am Theatre BETHUNE. R.C.'s attended service 10.30 am Church BETHUNE	[illeg]
BETHUNE	11.9.16		Company supplied party of 50 O.R. to C.R.E. Remainder of Company in billets training	[illeg]

2449 Wt. W14957/M90. 750,000 1/16 J.B.C.&A. Forms/C.2118/12.

WAR DIARY or INTELLIGENCE SUMMARY 14th Machine Gun Coy

Army Form C. 2118.

(Erase heading not required.)

Place	Date	Hour	Summary of Events and Information	Remarks and references to Appendices
BETHUNE	12.9.16		G.O.C 14th Infantry Bde inspected Coy transport lines E.17.B.8.8. at 12 noon. Company in billets training	
BETHUNE	13.9.16		Company in billets training	
BETHUNE	14.9.16		"	
BETHUNE	15.9.16		Company relieved the 96th Machine Gun Coy in the line (CAMBRIN SECTOR) as follows: "C" Section took out 3 positions in the FRONT LINE and 1 position in VILLAGE LINE near M.G. Headquarters. "D" Section took over positions 5 to 8 inclusive	

Army Form C. 2118.

WAR DIARY
or
INTELLIGENCE SUMMARY

(Erase heading not required.)

Place	Date	Hour	Summary of Events and Information	Remarks and references to Appendices
BETHUNE BEUVRY	15.9.16	contd	In "OLD BOOTS TRENCH. "A" Section took over positions 1 & 4 implacent (Nos 1 & 2 in REDOUBT, No 3 on RAILWAY, No 4 OLD BOOTS TRENCH) B Section in reserve ANNEQUIN. July complied 6 p.m.	
BEUVRY	16.9.16		Company (less 1 section in reserve ANNEQUIN) in trenches CAMBRIN SECTOR. 1 O.R. killed by splinter from own shell. 3.30 p.m. whilst on sentry duty at 19.2.78 52.17 Situation normal.	
BEUVRY	17.9.16		Company (less 1 section in reserve ANNEQUIN) in trenches CAMBRIN SECTOR Situation normal.	

WAR DIARY
or
INTELLIGENCE SUMMARY of 3rd Robert ? Cpy

(Erase heading not required.)

Army Form C. 2118.

Instructions regarding War Diaries and Intelligence Summaries are contained in F.S. Regs., Part II. and the Staff Manual respectively. Title Pages will be prepared in manuscript.

Place	Date	Hour	Summary of Events and Information	Remarks and references to Appendices
BEUVRY	18.9.16		Working Pty 16 in NW 1.20.d.30 Company (less 1 section in reserve ANNEQUIN) in trenches CAMBRIN SECTOR. Situation normal.	
BEUVRY	19.9.16		do	
BEUVRY	20.9.16		Company (less 1 section in reserve ANNEQUIN) in trenches CAMBRIN SECTOR. Situation normal. Lieut F.B. COWEN joined company (to command) from 149/M.S.Coy. Authority 149/ME 30 = S.C.75 dated 12.9.16	

WAR DIARY or INTELLIGENCE SUMMARY

Army Form C. 2118.

Place	Date	Hour	Summary of Events and Information	Remarks and references to Appendices
BEUVRY	21.9.16		The following reliefs took place:- "B" Section had just now relieved "C" section in FRONT LINE & VILLAGE LINE. "C" Section on relief, relieved "D" Section in junction 5 to 8 inclusive in "OLD BOOTS TRENCH" "D" Section on relief, relieved "A" Section in junctions 1 to 4 inclusive. (N°s 3 & 2 in REDOUBT N°3 on RAILWAY, N°4 in OLD BOOTS TRENCH, Detachment in "A" in MIDDLESEX & LITTLE ANNEQUIN Company (less 1 section in reserve ANNEQUIN) in trenches, CAMBRIN SECTOR. Situation normal.	
BEUVRY	22.9.16		LIEUT. F.B. COWAN reconnoitred ground for new Intermediate M.G. positions at night. Report for suggested positions to be prepared. M.Gs starting to work on positions…	

WAR DIARY
or
INTELLIGENCE SUMMARY

Army Form C. 2118.

(Erase heading not required.)

Place	Date	Hour	Summary of Events and Information	Remarks and references to Appendices
BEUVRY	22.9.16		Sortol divided up/m	
BEUVRY	23.9.16		Company (less 1 section in rear of ANNEQUIN) in trenches CAMBRIN SECTOR. LIEUT E. WIGLEY, 2/LT F.B. COWEN reconnoitred ground with view to selecting firing M.G. positions to deal with suggested operations at some future date. Got parties to work on TRENCH A27 CRS. 95. Positions decided upon. 1 O.R. wounded by shell. OLD BOOTS TRENCH A27 CRS.95. VICKERS M.GUN & 2 Rifles damaged by shell A27 CRS.95.	
BEUVRY	24.9.16		Company distributed as on Sept 23rd 1916. Weather normal. LIEUT F.B. COWEN went round new position with G.O.C. 2nd & Lt E. WIGLEY to command 14B Company, went to the comp. baff. article on employing V.G.S 16/9/16 (Reference 3rd Div.R Signed 2nd July 1916 (forwarded) 2nd July 1916 Ref 33Q.R.O.1475)	

WAR DIARY or INTELLIGENCE SUMMARY

Army Form C. 2118.

(Erase heading not required.)

Place	Date	Hour	Summary of Events and Information	Remarks and references to Appendices
BEUVRY	25.9.16		Company distributed as on 24 inst. Lieut F.B. Cowan received orders to attend conference at H.Q. 2nd Bn. Hampshire Regt in connection with raid to be arranged out.	
BEUVRY	26.9.16		The following reliefs took place. "A" section relieved "B" section in FRONT LINE and 1 gun in VILLAGE LINE. "B" section on relief, relieved "C" section in front line 3 to 5 inclusive in OKO BOOTS TRENCH. "C" section on relief relieved "D" section on frontage 1 to 4 inclusive (N°s 142 to 2000015	

WAR DIARY or INTELLIGENCE SUMMARY

Army Form C. 2118.

Place	Date	Hour	Summary of Events and Information	Remarks and references to Appendices
BEURY	26.9.16		No 3 on Railway, No 4 in OLD BOOTS TRENCH. "D" section on relief interlines to billets ANNEQUIN. Relief complete 1.30 p.m.	
,,	26.9.16		Received 21 Bn. Manchester Regt Junction orders reporting to rail. Built two new platforms in front line to fire on enemy suspected machine guns on flanks of Lonely party. Issued special orders to M.G. supporters as on the 25th inst.	
BEURY	27.9.16		Company distributed as on the 25th inst. Situation normal.	

WAR DIARY
or
INTELLIGENCE SUMMARY

Army Form C. 2118.

Place	Date	Hour	Summary of Events and Information	Remarks and references to Appendices
Beaury	28.9.16		Company distributed as on the 27th inst. Shell carried out. Two guns in new positions in front slept reducing enemy Machine gun with their fire	Capt Ryles M.V. 45000
Beaury	29.9.16		Company distributed as on the 28th inst. Situation normal	
Beaury	30.9.16		Company distributed as on the 29th inst. Situation normal	
				McConnor Lieut 14th Machine Gun Cy Comdg 14th Machine Gun Cy

14th Brigade.

32nd Division.

--- -----

14th BRIGADE MACHINE GUN COMPANY

OCTOBER 1 9 1 6

Army Form C. 2118

WAR DIARY
or
INTELLIGENCE SUMMARY

(Erase heading not required.)

14th Machine Gun Coy

By Lieutenant N.G.L. Mc000 (1353 N.E. 1/20,000)

Place	Date	Hour	Summary of Events and Information	Remarks and references to Appendices
BEUVRY	October 1st 1916		Company (less one section in Reserve Annequin) in trenches Cambrin Sector. Situation normal.	night
BEUVRY	2.10.16		"	night
BEUVRY & BETHUNE	3.10.16		Company relieved in the line Cambrin Section by 97th Machine Gun Company. Relief completed 2-50 p.m. After relief Company withdrew to billets BETHUNE.	night
BETHUNE	4.10.16		Company in billets training.	night
BETHUNE	5.10.16		"	night

Army Form C. 2118.

WAR DIARY
or
INTELLIGENCE SUMMARY 14 E. Machine Gun Coy
(Erase heading not required.)

Appendix 36 N o 1 110 000

Place	Date	Hour	Summary of Events and Information	Remarks and references to Appendices
BETHUNE	6.10.16		Company in billets training	Sgd
BETHUNE	7.10.16		Company attended Church Parades as follows :- C of E. Parade Service 9-15 a.m. at Theatre BETHUNE. R.C.'s Mass Parade at 10-30 a.m. at BETHUNE Cathedral. Presbyterian Parade Service 10 a.m. in Tobacco factory BETHUNE.	Sgd
BETHUNE	8.10.16		Company in billets training	Sgd
BETHUNE	9.10.16		Do	Sgd

Army Form C. 2118.

WAR DIARY
INTELLIGENCE SUMMARY 1/4 E Machine Gun Coy

(Erase heading not required.)

Instructions regarding War Diaries and Intelligence Summaries are contained in F.S. Regs., Part II. and the Staff Manual respectively. Title Pages will be prepared in manuscript.

Place	Date	Hour	Summary of Events and Information	Remarks and references to Appendices
BETHUNE. BUSNES	10.10.16		Company moved with 4th Infantry Bde to billets BUSNES. Route :— Cross Roads E.3.d.7.7. CHOCQUES, Point D.5.3.9.0. — BESNETTES, Point V.3.d.4.4. passing starting point Cross Roads E.7.7. at 10.15 a.m. Arrived in billets BUSNES at 1-5 p.m.	Ref Sheets 36ᵃ 36ᵇ 1/40,000
BUSNES	11.10.16		Company in billets training.	
BUSNES	12.10.16		do	
BUSNES	13.10.16		do	
BUSNES	14.10.16		Company took part in a Brigade Tactical Exercise 9.30 a.m. to 1 p.m.	Ref Sheets 1/40,000 36ᵃ 51/100,000 Sheets 5 & 11
			2nd Lieut C.H. THEW evacuated to C.C.S.	
			2nd Lieut R.W. BURTON proceeded to M.G. Depot GRANTHAM.	

WAR DIARY or INTELLIGENCE SUMMARY

Army Form C. 2118.

4th Cheshire Field Company

(Erase heading not required.)

Place	Date	Hour	Summary of Events and Information	Remarks and references to Appendices
BUSNES.	15.10.16		Company moved with 14th Infantry Brigade into the RAIMBERT area. Route via LILLERS – BURBURE having starting point Road Junction 18–35 at 10–13 a.m. arriving in billets RAIMBERT at 1–5 p.m.	Appx
RAIMBERT.				
RAIMBERT. ROCOURT. ST LAURENT.	16.10.16		Company moved with 14th Infantry Brigade into the area BAILLEUL – AUX – CORNAILLES – ST MICHAEL. Route via PERNES VAL HOUIN – BRAYAS clearing OSTERVILLE by noon. Head of Company having starting point Cross Roads 330 yards West of PERNES at 8.25 a.m. Tail at Cross Roads 900 yards West of PERNES at 8.45 a.m. arrived in billets ROCOURT – ST LAURENT at 11.35 a.m.	Appx
ROCOURT. ST LAURENT. REBREUVE.	17.10.16		Company moved with 14th Infantry Brigade to REBREUVE. Route via BONEVILLE MONCHEUX – HOUVIN – HOUVIGNEUL – CANETTEMONT. Head of Company (having starting point Cross Roads 900 yards West of Junct of Manisnil – St Pol at 9.15 a.m.) A tactical scheme was performed on the march. Company arrived in billets REBREUVE 3–30 p.m.	Appx

WAR DIARY
INTELLIGENCE SUMMARY

Army Form C. 2118.

(Erase heading not required.)

Place	Date	Hour	Summary of Events and Information	Remarks and references to Appendices
REBREUVE BEAUVAL	18.10.16		Company moved with 14 Infantry Brigade to Beauval. Route via LUCHEUX - DOULLENS (CHURCH IVERGY 8.28am.) arriving in billets Beauval 2-15 p.m.	
BEAUVAL	19.10.16		Company whilst on the march to Warloy with 14 Infantry Bde received orders at 10 a.m. to return to billets Beauval. Company arrived in billets Beauval 11 a.m.	
BEAUVAL	20.10.16		Company in billets training. Sect. C. M. Singer rejoined company from 1st Corps Rest camp.	
BEAUVAL	21.10.16		Company with 14 Infantry Bde moved to Warloy via BERNAVESNE-PUCHEVILLERS-TOUTENCOURT-VADENCOURT having starting point road junction just E. of CHURCH BEAUVAL at 10-15am. arriving in billets Warloy 3-20 p.m. 3.0. R proceeded to M.G. Base Depot for further instruction. Lieut C. Birchall } joined by from M.G. Base Depot. A. Barrold }	

Army Form C. 2118.

WAR DIARY
of
INTELLIGENCE SUMMARY 14th Machine Gun Company

(Erase heading not required.)

Instructions regarding War Diaries and Intelligence Summaries are contained in F. S. Regs., Part II. and the Staff Manual respectively. Title Pages will be prepared in manuscript.

Place	Date	Hour	Summary of Events and Information	Remarks and references to Appendices
WARLOY	22.10.16		Map reference 1/40,000 & 1/20,000 S.E. 1/20,000 C/E Church Warloy 11 a.m.	
WARLOY	23.10.16		Company with 14th Infantry Bde moved to billets BRICKFIELDS area on the BOUZINCOURT ALBERT Road. Route HENENCOURT MILLENCOURT ALBERT, having starting point Road Junction 200 yds S. 26.f.3 and WARLOY-BAIZIEUX B27 a.3.8. 3.10 p.m. arriving in billets BRICKFIELDS area 6.27 a.3.8. 3.10 p.m. C.S.M. PEARSON proceeded to Cadet School G.H.Q. BLANGERQUES to join Infantry Coy.	
BRICKFIELDS BOUZINCOURT ALBERT ROAD	24.10.16		Company in billets awaiting orders. 2/Lieut A.L. HYSLOP rejoined Company from leave U.K. (Weather Wet) N° 16453 Sergt. H. HALL took over duties of C.S.M.	

Army Form C. 2118.

WAR DIARY
or
INTELLIGENCE SUMMARY [illegible unit name]

(Erase heading not required.)

Instructions regarding War Diaries and Intelligence Summaries are contained in F. S. Regs., Part II. and the Staff Manual respectively. Title Pages will be prepared in manuscript.

Place	Date	Hour	Summary of Events and Information	Remarks and references to Appendices
BRICKFIELDS BOUZINCOURT ALBERT ROAD.	25.10.16		Company awaiting orders. Weather wet.	
BRICKFIELDS BOUZINCOURT ALBERT ROAD.	26.10.16		Company moved with 14 Infantry Bde to HARPONVILLE via BOUZINCOURT - SENLIS - VADENCOURT, arriving in billets HARPONVILLE 3-45 p.m.	
HARPONVILLE	27.10.16		Company in billets training. Weather wet. I.O.P. seconded to G.H.Q.S.	
HARPONVILLE	28.10.16		Company in billets training. Weather wet.	

2449 Wt. W14957/M90 750,000 1/16 J.B.C. & A. Forms/C.2118/12.

WAR DIARY or INTELLIGENCE SUMMARY

Army Form C. 2118.

Place	Date	Hour	Summary of Events and Information	Remarks and references to Appendices
HARPONVILLE	28.10.16		C/E Church Parade 2.30 p.m.	
HARPONVILLE	29.10.16		Company took part in a Brigade Tactical Exercise 9.0 a.m. to 11 a.m. Weather Wet.	
HARPONVILLE	30.10.16		Company in billets training. Night scheme carried out by Coy 6 p.m. to 7.30 p.m.	
HARPONVILLE	31.10.16		Company on Brigade Tactical scheme 9.30 a.m. to 12.30 p.m.	

14th Machine Gun Coy.

Operation Order No 8

Albert 2nd Dec 1916

① DUTIES

Orderly Officer tomorrow
                Lieut C. Birrell.

Next for duty
                2/Lieut M. Givens

Section on duty tomorrow
                "C" Section.

Next for duty "D"

② MOVES

Company will move to Brickfields area or
BOUZINCOURT ALBERT ROAD tomorrow.
Head of Company will pass starting
point (Road Junction 200yds S.W. of B in
WARLOY BAILLON) at 12.51 p.m.
Order of March A.B.C.D.
Transport will move as a whole in rear
of Company.
Dress Marching order without packs.
Packs will be carried on limbers.
Limbers to be loaded and covers tied
down by 12-30 p.m.

③ PARADE

Company will parade in Road in front
of Billets at 12-30 p.m. ready to
move off at 12-49 p.m.

④ VALISES BLANKETS

Officers Valises and Blankets will
be at Q.M. Stores by 11-30 a.m.

⑤ BILLETING PARTY

Lieut C.M. Sugden with 3 cyclist
Orderlies (to be detailed by Sergt
Major) will report to Commandant
Brickfields area at W.27.A.3.8 by
12 noon tomorrow to take over billets.

⑥ TRANSFERS

No 16820 Pte Jones A is transferred
from D Section to C Section
No 4330 Pte McAllister is
transferred from Transport to "A" Section

⑦ POSTING

No 16791 C.S.M. Pearson, J. proceeds tomorrow to Cadet School BLENDECQUES.

No 16425 Sergt Hall, H will take over the duties of Company Sergeant Major from tomorrow.

⑧ STRENGTH

No 16249 Pte Austin, P. having been evacuated to C.C.S. 19.10.16 is struck off the Strength of this Company accordingly.

⑨ CENSORSHIP

All ranks are forbidden to disclose in any letter the Brigade, Division or any other formation to which their own or any other unit belongs, unless it forms a necessary part of that Unit's address.

This applies equally to the address on the envelope and the contents of the letter. (Ref 32 Div R.O. 1505)

⑩ ARMS AND ACCOUTREMENTS - WOUNDED AND SICK SOLDIERS

It has been customary for a man who is wounded, however slightly, to remove all his equipment, leave it in the trench or on the ground, and then go to the Regimental Aid Post. The result of this practice is that a very large amount of equipment is lost or destroyed.

All slightly wounded men will bring their arms and equipment with them and retain possession of them until they are handed in at the Casualty Clearing Station.
(Res Reserve Army R.O. 17 dated October 19th. 1916)

28/10/16

Capt.
OC. 14th Machine Gun Coy

C. O.
14 th Machine Gun Coy.

14th Brigade.

32nd Division.

14th BRIGADE MACHINE GUN COMPANY

NOVEMBER 1 9 1 6

WAR DIARY
or
INTELLIGENCE SUMMARY. 14 Machine Gun Coy

Army Form C. 2118.

Ref Sheet 57° 1/40,000

Place	Date	Hour	Summary of Events and Information	Remarks and references to Appendices
HARPONVILLE	1.11.16		Company in billets training.	(Sgd) W.R. Bagnall Lt
HARPONVILLE	2.11.16		"	(Sgd) W.R. Bagnall Lt
HARPONVILLE	3.11.16		"	(Sgd) W.R. Bagnall Lt
HARPONVILLE	4.11.16		"	(Sgd) W.R. Bagnall Lt
HARPONVILLE	5.11.16		Company attended Church Parade as follows:— C of E. Service 12 NOON. Presbyterian " 12 NOON. R.C. " 9 A.M.	(Sgd) W.R. Bagnall Lt

Army Form C. 2118.

WAR DIARY
or
INTELLIGENCE SUMMARY. 114th Machine Gun Coy.

(Erase heading not required.)

Place	Date	Hour	Summary of Events and Information	Remarks and references to Appendices
HARPONVILLE.	6.11.16		Company in billets training.	(Rollie Russell) Capt
HARPONVILLE.	7.11.16		" "	(Rollie Russell) Capt
HARPONVILLE.	8.11.16		1.O.R. proceeded on leave to U.K.	(Rollie Russell) Capt
HARPONVILLE.	9.11.16		A & B Sections took part in 114th Bde. tactical attack on training ground HARPONVILLE. 9.30 a.m. to 1 p.m.	(Rollie Russell) Capt
HARPONVILLE.	10.11.16		Company in billets training.	(Rollie Russell) Capt

Army Form C. 2118.

WAR DIARY
or
INTELLIGENCE SUMMARY. /4th Machine Gun Coy.

(Erase heading not required.)

Place	Date	Hour	Summary of Events and Information	Remarks and references to Appendices
HARPONVILLE 1.11.16			Company in billets training	J. Talbot 57. L/40.000 (signature)
HARPONVILLE 12.11.16			Company in billets training. Brigade inspected Company Transport at 12 noon. 4.O.R. proceeded to Eterpegny TANKS ACHEUX 7.O.R.'s 5/6 Royal Scots. 3.O.R.'s 10th Dorsets. 4.O.R.'s 2nd Northumberland. 1.O.R. 15th H.L.I. } Attached to Coy for duty.	(signature)
HARPONVILLE V.12.c.7. & 13.11.16			Company moved to billets V.12.c.7. & Routevia YBRENCOURT - WARLOY - SENLIS - VARENNES- HEDAUVILLE ROAD leaving starting journey Road Junction U.21.a.3.4. at 10.15 A.M. arriving in billets V.12.c.7.8. at 12.40 P.M.	(signature)

Army Form C. 2118.

WAR DIARY

INTELLIGENCE SUMMARY. 14th Machine Gun Coy.

(Erase heading not required.)

Instructions regarding War Diaries and Intelligence Summaries are contained in F. S. Regs., Part II. and the Staff Manual respectively. Title pages will be prepared in manuscript.

Place	Date	Hour	Summary of Events and Information	Remarks and references to Appendices
V.12.c.	7.8.14.11.16		Company awaiting orders for impending operations. C.O. Stokefoot offered and C.Q.M.S. attended experiment in conveying rations on pack mules by 1st Dorset Regt. and 2nd Manchester Regt. at rationed transport lines at 11 a.m.	Ref Sheet 57 d 1.40.000 (Miller Brady)
V.62.c. 7.8 MAILLET MAILLET	15.11.16		Company moved up to tribes in MAILLET-MAILLET preparatory to going into the line the following day.	Ref Sheet 57 M
MAILLET MAILLET	16.11.16		The Company moved up into the line south of SERRE from MAILLET-MAILLET at 6 A.M. Relief was not finished in day light owing to enemy observation. At 6 P.M. 6 guns moved, 2 Lt. A.L. HYSLOP and 2 guns moved, 2 Lt. M. LATHAM went up to take over positions from the 6th & 9th Coys. the 5 guns being attached to the H.H. on the left and the 2 guns to the 2nd MANCHESTER Regt. on the right. There was much efficiency in carrying over to the newly captured trenches owing to enemy barrage, but position occupied. No casualties.	R.A. Hyslop Lt.

A.5834. Wt. W4973/M687. 750,000. 8/16. D.D.&L., Ltd. Forms/C.2118/13.

WAR DIARY

INTELLIGENCE SUMMARY 1st Machine Gun Coy

Army Form C. 2118.

Place	Date	Hour	Summary of Events and Information	Remarks and references to Appendices
MAILLEY MAILLET	17.11.16		Spent in consolidating the line, building up positions, and general reconnaissance. In the evening one gun of A Section was sent up to reinforce 2/Lt H. LATHAM. Unfortunately the gun and crew were knocked out by shell fire in 6.3. HEBUTERNE as it was coming into action. 2 O.R.s being killed and 4 O.R.s wounded. Enemy shelled most of the day, with heavy barrage during the afternoon.	57d 1:40,000 6.3.HEBUTERNE 2/c
MAILLEY MAILLET	18.11.16	6.10 AM	At 6.10 AM the 15th H.L.I. and 2nd MANCHES. REGT attacked and took their objectives, 4 guns going with the H.L.I. and 2 with the MANCHES. REGT. Unfortunately the 2nd MAN. REGT. with 2 machine guns under 2/Lt H. LATHAM pushed on too far and were cut off by the enemy, nothing having been heard of them since the information being passed back by Lt. BIRCHALL as that was an went over. Rest of 4 guns attacked to the H.L.I. under 2/Lt. Here hardly been in any counter attacks. Two guns attacked in sub-action at 7-10 AM Point L85	a.27.A.5.2. 2/A

1/Lt. HYSLOP

WAR DIARY

INTELLIGENCE SUMMARY

Army Form C. 2118.

Place	Date	Hour	Summary of Events and Information	Remarks and references to Appendices
See	16/11/16 (cont)		being fired at the enemy 500 strong, who were advancing on the open (at about 600 yards range). The fire was most effective, there being many casualties amongst the enemy and their advance stopped immediately. In co-operation with the artillery firing 4 guns were opened. I Lt. O. BENTLEY opened intense overhead fire at 6.18 a.m. on an artillery barrage lifted from the trenches from line of his support. The tripods and enemy strong points and ranges from 1800 x to 2200 x. 15,000 rounds being fired. I of the enemy air force the LUCKNOW CAV. M.G. SQUADRON were attached to no. 3 enemy guns were employed in overhead fire across his front S of TREE ALLEY in conjunction with the 11 guns under 2 Lt. O. BENTLEY. These guns fired at intervals throughout the night.	

WAR DIARY or INTELLIGENCE SUMMARY

Army Form C. 2118.

14th Machine Gun Coy.

Place	Date	Hour	Summary of Events and Information	Remarks and references to Appendices
MAILLEY MAILLET	16.11.16 (cont.)		Ref. Sheet 57d 1/40,000. 20,000 rounds heavy fire, fire was reported by our troops in the front line as being effective. Hostile M.G. and rifle fire being kept down to a minimum. (1 Officer and 16 O.R. of enemy were taken prisoners by one of the gun teams under Sergt. BOON)	
MAILLEY MAILLET	19.11.16		Day spent in improving gun positions in line. In evening 4 guns under 2 Lt O.BENTLEY relieved 4 guns under 2 Lt AL HYSLOP, the relieved teams being in somewhat exhausted condition. Bar dark till dawn of the 20th overhead fire from reserve guns was carried out. Previous evening 18,000 rds. being fired	R.L.H.Sh. H.
MAILLEY MAILLET	20.11.16		Consolidating line and overhead fire from dusk till dawn the following night. An average number of rounds about fired per team 10,000.	R.L.H.Sh. H.
MAILLEY MAILLET	28.11.16		The 16th NORTHUMBERLAND F's attacked enemy strong point SE at 5 am. Our guns under 2nd Lt R.L.H.Sh. O.BENTLEY and under Lt. BIRKETT covered enemy's enemy fire to keep unfortunate ...ction were unsuccessful owing to the much the evening the MGs of 2/DOWN C.M. S.DW.	R.L.H.Sh. H.

WAR DIARY

of 114th Machine Gun Coy

INTELLIGENCE SUMMARY.

(Erase heading not required.)

Army Form C. 2118.

Place	Date	Hour	Summary of Events and Information	Remarks and references to Appendices
Ref Sheet 57d 1/40,000				
	23.11.16 (cont.)		returned to the 3rd Div.	
	24.11.16		We were relieved at 10 PM by the 20th Coy — the relief being carried out without difficulty — the 20th Coy reported there was little or no enemy shelling.	R24.Sd.5
	General Remarks		We found that the emergency cases were useless and pivotating through tongues are this difficulty guns were wrapped up in the mens waterproof sheets as this was found to be the easiest way. We also found that 1 NCO & 6 men were absolutely making use, for personnel of Gun team, to assist spectators, all these men being employed in carrying up ammn, tripods etc. No men being left for carrying water, any rations for the teams. The rationing of the team up in the front was found to be satisfactory, as one Other personnel of the reserve were carrying up and indented for. (There were used as ration parties.)	A.Webb Lt.

Army Form C. 2118.

WAR DIARY
of
INTELLIGENCE SUMMARY. 14th Machine Gun Coy
(Erase heading not required.)

Place	Date	Hour	Summary of Events and Information	Remarks and references to Appendices
MAILLY MAILLET	25.11.16		Company personnel moved by bus to billets AUTHIEULE arriving 5.30 p.m. Transport moved under Lieut J. BARKANY 2nd R. Innis Fus in rear of 96th Machine Gun Coy having starting point Road Junction R.18 C.8.2 at 9 a.m. Route:- HEDAUVILLE - ACHEUX - LOUVENCOURT - MARIEUX, then leaving 96th Infantry Brigade under 2nd Lieut R.R. MATTHEWS via BEAUQUESNE to BEAUVAL. 2nd Lieut R.R. Matthews then received orders from O.C. to join company at AUTHIEULE.	Ref Sheet 57dSW 1/100,000 Ref Billets AUTHIEULE (signed)
AUTHIEULE PERNOIS 26.11.16 (HALLOY)			Company moved to billets PERNOIS HALLOY having starting point Road Junction 660 yards W. of D in DOULLENS at 10-10 a.m. Route:- 500 yds N. of D in CITADELLE - H & M - FIENVILLERS - CROSS ROADS 3/4 mile N. of NUN - BERNEUIL - CANAPLES arriving PERNOIS HALLOY at 4.15 p.m. Lieut C.M. SINGER proceeded to GRANTHAM.	(signed)

Army Form C. 2118.

WAR DIARY
or of
INTELLIGENCE SUMMARY. 1st & 2nd Machine Gun Company

(Erase heading not required.)

Place	Date	Hour	Summary of Events and Information	Remarks and references to Appendices
PERNOIS HALLOY	27.11.16		Company in billets training. Lieut C.A.G.S. Sim proceeded to Grantham.	[signature]
PERNOIS HALLOY	28.11.16		Company in billets training. 2nd Lieut O.Bentley and 5 O.R. proceeded on leave to U.K.	[signature]
PERNOIS HALLOY	29.11.16		Company in billets training.	[signature]
PERNOIS HALLOY	30.11.16		2nd Lieut R.G.H.D. Fairbarns } Joined Company from M.G. " G.M.B. Reed } Base Depot.	[signature]
				Charles Rinshall Ryt Capt.

14th Brigade
32nd Division.

14th BRIGADE MACHINE GUN COMPANY

DECEMBER 1916

WAR DIARY OF

14 MGC Vol XI

Army Form C. 2118.

INTELLIGENCE SUMMARY. 141 Machine Gun Company

Ref Sheet LENS II. 1/100.000.

Place	Date	Hour	Summary of Events and Information	Remarks and references to Appendices
HALLOY.	1.12.16		Company in billets training.	O'Brute ¼
HALLOY.	2.12.16		" "	O'Brute ¼
HALLOY.	3.12.16		Church Parades.	O'Brute ¼
HALLOY.	4.12.16		Company in billets training.	O'Brute ¼
HALLOY.	5.12.16		B.O.R.s Reinforcements joined company from Machine Gun Base Depot CAMIERS.	O'Brute ¼
HALLOY.	6.12.16		Company in billets training.	O'Brute ¼
HALLOY.	7.12.16		2nd Lieut M.G.STEVENS and 3.O.R.s proceeded on leave to U.K.	O'Brute ¼
HALLOY.	8.12.16		141 Infantry Bde inspected by Corps General. Brathers tack.	O'Brute ¼
HALLOY.	9.12.16		Company in billets training.	O'Brute ¼

Army Form C. 2118.

WAR DIARY of
INTELLIGENCE SUMMARY. 114/ Machine Gun Company

(Erase heading not required.)

Instructions regarding War Diaries and Intelligence Summaries are contained in F. S. Regs., Part II. and the Staff Manual respectively. Title pages will be prepared in manuscript.

Place	Date	Hour	Summary of Events and Information	Remarks and references to Appendices
HALLOY.	10.12.16		Ref/ Sheet LENS 11.1:100.000. Church Parades. 2nd Lieut O. BENTLEY and 3 O.R.s from leave U.K.	O Bentley Lt 3/5
HALLOY.	11.12.16		Company in billets training. 17 O.R.s Reinforcements joined Company from Machine Gun Corps Base Depot CAMIERS. 1 Light Draught Horse shot by Capt ANDERSON A.V.C. Veterinary Reserves. 1 O.R. from leave U.K.	O Bentley 3/5
HALLOY.	12.12.16		Company in billets training.	O Bentley Lt 3/5
HALLOY.	13.12.16		1 O.R. from leave U.K.	O Bentley Lt 3/5
HALLOY.	14.12.16		Company on Village Defence Scheme N. of HALLOY. from 9-45 a.m. to 1-0 p.m.	O Bentley Lt 3/5

Army Form C. 2118.

WAR DIARY

of 14/ Machine Gun Company

INTELLIGENCE SUMMARY

(Erase heading not required.)

Place	Date	Hour	Summary of Events and Information	Remarks and references to Appendices
			Ref Sheet LENS II 1/100.000	
HALLOY.	15.12.16		Company in billets training. I.O.R. evacuated to No 3 Australian C.C.S.	Stansbury Mr
HALLOY.	16.12.16		Company in billets training. 4 O.R.s proceeded to leave U.K.	Stansbury Mr
HALLOY.	17.12.16		Church Parade. 2.O.R.s rejoined Company from M.G. Base CAMIERS.	Stansbury Mr
HALLOY.	18.12.16		Company on route march with 14/ Infantry Bde via Starting Point Bridge over Stream at LE-SOUDET. 9.30 a.m. - BERTEAUCOURT - LES-DAMES - ST LEGER - DOMART - BERNEUIL - CANAPLES - PERNOIS - 1.50 p.m.	Stansbury Mr

Army Form C. 2118.

WAR DIARY
or
INTELLIGENCE SUMMARY.   14/ Machine Gun Coy
(Erase heading not required)

Place	Date	Hour	Summary of Events and Information	Remarks and references to Appendices
HALLOY.	18.12.16		Ref Sheet LENS. 1/100,000. Search made for Robert Bicycles in Company billets by Lieutenant C. B. ROHAN, and a Nil report rendered to 41/ Infantry Bde. H.Q. 1.O.R. rejoined Company from No 3 Australian C.C.S.	Cloudy 7/15 Cloudy 8/15
HALLOY.	19.12.16		Company in billets training.	Cloudy 9/15
HALLOY.	20.12.16		New Small Box Respirators issued to Company and instructions re fitting were given by Section Officers who had attended class at Divisional Gas School CANADRES. Lieut. A. BLOOMFIELD joined Company from 105 M.G. Company. Appointed 2no in Command. 2nd Lieut. M. GIVENS > 1.O.R. rejoined Coy from leave, U.K.	

A.8834. Wt. W4973/M687. 730,000. 8/16. D. D. & L. Ltd. Forms/C.2118/13.

Army Form C. 2118.

WAR DIARY

INTELLIGENCE SUMMARY 114 Machine Gun Company

(Erase heading not required.)

Place	Date	Hour	Summary of Events and Information	Remarks and references to Appendices
HALLOY	21.12.16		Rd Sheet LENS 11. 1/100.000 Company on tactical scheme 9.0 a.m 1.0 p.m. 1.0.R. mounted to C.C.S. and start off the strength accordingly.	McDonough 2/Lt
HALLOY	22.12.16		Whole Company (except men absent with wire party fitted with small Box Respirators and same were tested in Gas Chamber (Bullet 109 PERNOIS) under the supervision of Divisional Gas Officer.	McDonough 2/Lt
HALLOY	23.12.16		Company in billets during Section Officers on Brigade tactical scheme from 9.30 a.m. - 1.45 p.m.	McDonough 2/Lt

Army Form C. 2118.

WAR DIARY
or
INTELLIGENCE SUMMARY
141 Machine Gun Company

(Erase heading not required.)

Instructions regarding War Diaries and Intelligence Summaries are contained in F. S. Regs., Part II. and the Staff Manual respectively. Title pages will be prepared in manuscript.

Place	Date	Hour	Summary of Events and Information	Remarks and references to Appendices
HALLOY	24.12.16		Sgnme Hennes. 2.O.R. proceeded on leave to U.K.	Sgt Sheet-Lewis M. 1/100,000
HALLOY	25.12.16		" "	
HALLOY	26.12.16		Company in billets training. 2nd Lieut A.L. HYSLOP and 2.O.R. proceeded to Machine Gun School Camiers for course of instruction in Machine Gun. & 1.O.R. Bolton.	
HALLOY	27.12.16		Company on Route March via. HALLOY- BERTEAUCOURT - VIGNACOURT. 9.15am to 1 p.m. Captain E. WIGLEY proceeded on leave to U.K.	

Army Form C. 2118.

WAR DIARY
or
INTELLIGENCE SUMMARY.

141 Machine Gun Coy

(Erase heading not required.)

Place	Date	Hour	Summary of Events and Information	Remarks and references to Appendices
HALLOY	28.12.16		Company on Tactical Scheme (Formation and use of Ground) between BOIS-de-ST LEGER and BOIS DE DOMART) from 9.0 a.m to 12.30pm. 3 O.R.s reinforcements joined Company from Machine Gun Transport Depot ABBEVILLE.	By Shuttleworth 11/1/1962.000 Abbreviated list.
HALLOY	29.12.16		Company in billets training. Lieut A. BLOOMFIELD, Lieut C. BIRCHALL, 2nd Lieut O. BENTLEY, 2nd Lieut A.H.D. FAIRBAIRNS attended Brigade Tactical Scheme for Officers. 1. O.R. rejoined Company from leave U.K.	Abbreviated list.

Army Form C. 2118.

WAR DIARY
INTELLIGENCE SUMMARY.

141/ Machine Gun Company

(Erase heading not required.)

Instructions regarding War Diaries and Intelligence Summaries are contained in F. S. Regs., Part II and the Staff Manual respectively. Title pages will be prepared in manuscript.

Place	Date	Hour	Summary of Events and Information	Remarks and references to Appendices
HALLOY	30.12.16		Brigade Tactical Scheme for troops cancelled. Company in billets training. 1 O.R. rejoined Company from I.B.D. 2 O.Rs proceeded on leave to U.K.	Bloomfield
HALLOY	31.12.16		Divine Services. Second fitting of new Box Respirators took place at 15/H.L.I. H.Q.	Bloomfield

D. Bloomfield Lieut
for O.C. 141st M.G. Coy

Army Form C. 2118.

WAR DIARY
or
INTELLIGENCE SUMMARY. 14th Machine Gun Coy.

Vol 1.

(Erase heading not required.)

Instructions regarding War Diaries and Intelligence Summaries are contained in F. S. Regs. Part II. and the Staff Manual respectively. Title pages will be prepared in manuscript.

Place	Date	Hour	Summary of Events and Information	Remarks and references to Appendices
			Ref. Sheet LENS 11 1/70,000	
HALLOY	1-1-17		Company in billets training. 1.O.R. reinforcement joined Coy from M.G. Base Depot.	Abloomfield
HALLOY	2-1-17		"A", "B" and "C" Sections on Brigade Tactical Scheme 9.30am to 1.0 pm. All officers and transport Personnel of Coy attended lecture given by A.D.V.S. at billet No.19A BERTEAUCOURT. 5.30pm 1.O.R. returned to Coy from leave U.K.	Abloomfield
HALLOY	3-1-17		Coy on Route March via HALLOY – HAVERNAS – NAOURS – FRESSELLES 9.15am to 1.0pm. Lieut. A BLOOMFIELD, Lieut. C. BIRCHALL, 2/Lieut. O. BENTLEY, and 2/Lieut. R.R MATTHEWS visited the piers to Brigade taking over same. 30 R/s joined Coy from M.G. Base Depot.	Abloomfield
HALLOY	4-1-17		Company on Tactical Scheme (Defence) Ground N of HALLOY.	Abloomfield

Army Form C. 2118.

WAR DIARY
or
INTELLIGENCE SUMMARY

(Erase heading not required.)

14/ Cheshire Yeor Coy. R.E.

Ref. Sheets. LENS 1/200000
HEBUTERNE 1/10,000

Place	Date	Hour	Summary of Events and Information	Remarks and references to Appendices
HALLOY	5-1-17		Company in billets training. Lieut C. BIRCHALL to hospital.	
HALLOY BEAUVAL	6-1-17		Company moved with 14th Inf. Brigade to billets BEAUVAL via CANAPLES – MONTRELET arriving BEAUVAL 1-5 pm	
BEAUVAL COURCELLES	7-1-17		Company moved by bus to BUS-LES-ARTOIS and then marched to COURCELLES. "A" & "C" relieved 2 Sections of 8th M.G. Coy in the line in front of SERRE and portion of line held by left Brigade. Trenches and dug-outs in very bad condition. Company Transport Lines at BUS-LES-ARTOIS. Two Sections and Headquarters in billets COURCELLES.	
COURCELLES	9-1-17		"A" & "C" Sections in trenches. "B" & "D" " and Headquarters in billets COURCELLES. 1.O.R. killed by shell. CAPT. E. WIGLEY rejoined Coy from leave U.K.	

Army Form C. 2118.

WAR DIARY
or
INTELLIGENCE SUMMARY   14th Machine Gun Company

(Erase heading not required.)

Place	Date	Hour	Summary of Events and Information	Remarks and references to Appendices
COURCELLES	9-1-17		Ref. Sheets HEBUTERNE 10,000 5½D 40,000	
			A & C Sections in the line.	
			B & D " and Headquarters in billets COURCELLES.	
			Transport Lines at BUS-LES-ARTOIS.	
COURCELLES	10-1-17		A & C Sections in the line.	
			B & D " and Headquarters in billets COURCELLES.	
			Transport Lines at BUS-LES-ARTOIS.	
			1 Machine Gun to Ordnance for repair.	
			1 O.R. rejoined Coy from Base Signals.	
			1 O.R attached to Base Signals	
COURCELLES	11-1-17		Company relief took place, B & D Sections relieved A & C Sections in the line at night.	
			After relief A & C Sections marched to billets COURCELLES. 1 O.R. from leave U.K.	
COURCELLES	12-1-17		B and D Sections in the line.	
			A and C " and Headquarters in billets COURCELLES	
			Transport at BUS-LES-ARTOIS.	
			1 O.R. from leave U.K. 1 Officer to leave U.K.	

Army Form C. 2118.

WAR DIARY
or
INTELLIGENCE SUMMARY.   11th Machine Gun Company

(Erase heading not required.)

Ref sheet's HEBUTERNE 57d & 57b

Place	Date	Hour	Summary of Events and Information	Remarks and references to Appendices
COURCELLES	13-1-17		A & C Sections in billets COURCELLES. B & D " " in the line. Transport at BUS-LES-ARTOIS. 1 O.R. wounded by shell fire.	Woodroffe
COURCELLES	14-1-17		A & C Sections in billets COURCELLES B & D " " in the line Transport at BUS-LES-ARTOIS. 2 O.R.s to M.G. Corps CAMIERS	Woodroffe
COURCELLES	15-1-17		Company relief took place, A & C Sections relieved B & D in the line during the afternoon and evening. After relief B & D Sections withdrew to billets COURCELLES	Woodroffe
COURCELLES	16-1-17		B & D Sections in billets COURCELLES. A & C " " in the line. Transport lines at BUS-LES-ARTOIS. 1 Officer and 2 O.R. from M.G. Corps.	Woodroffe

Army Form C. 2118.

WAR DIARY
or
INTELLIGENCE SUMMARY 14th Machine Gun Company

(Erase heading not required.)

Ref Sheets HEBUTERNE 1/40,000
57D 51/D 7&1/20

Place	Date	Hour	Summary of Events and Information	Remarks and references to Appendices
COURCELLES	17-1-17		B + D Sections in billets COURCELLES. A + C " " in the line. Transport Lines at BUS-LES-ARTOIS.	
COURCELLES	18-1-17		B + D Sections in billets COURCELLES A + C " " in the line Transport at BUS-LES-ARTOIS 1 O.R from leave U.K 2.O.R'd to D° D° 2.O.R to M.G. Base Depot as incompetent for M.G. duties	
COURCELLES	19-1-17		A + C Sections were relieved by 2 Sections of 95th M.G. Coy. Relief complete 9.30 p.m. After relief A + C entrained to billets COURCELLES. "B" Section relieved 2 teams each of 20th and 22nd Coys. 2 in ELLIS SQUARE and 2 on REDAN RIDGE respectively. Relief complete 11-30 p.m. 1 Officer and 1 O.R. from C.C.S.	

Army Form C. 2118.

WAR DIARY
or
INTELLIGENCE SUMMARY
(Erase heading not required.)

1st M[achine] G[un] Squadron [Guards?]

Ref Sheets 57d N.W. 1/20,000
Sheets 57d 1/10,000
K.3 — M.21.

Place	Date	Hour	Summary of Events and Information	Remarks and references to Appendices
COURCELLES	20-1-17		"B" Section in the line. Sqn Headquarters, A, C & D Sections in billets COURCELLES. Transport at BUS-LES-ARTOIS	
COURCELLES MAILLY MAILLET	21-1-17		Company less "B" Section and Transport vacated billets at COURCELLES at 3 pm. and moved to billets MAILLY MAILLET arriving at 3-50 pm. Very good billets. Weather extremely cold.	
MAILLY MAILLET	22-1-17		"A" Section relieved 2 teams of 96th M.G. Coy on RIDGE — 2 teams of "B" Section at A & B positions on REDAN. 1 team of "B" at ELLIS SQUARE relieved 1 team of 96th Coy at LEGEND TRENCH. 2 teams of 19 Section from REDAN relieved 1 team at ELLIS SQUARE. The teams relieved by them proceeded to H.Q. billets MAILLY-MAILLET. Relief complete 12 midnight. Transport lines at BUS-LES-ARTOIS. "D" Section on tactical scheme with 1st DORSET. REGT.	

A.5834 Wt. W4973/M687 750m 8/16 D.D.&L. Ltd. Forms/C.2118/3

Army Form C. 2118.

WAR DIARY
or
INTELLIGENCE SUMMARY
(Erase heading not required.)

Army Form C. 2118.

1st Ch. Machine Gun Company

Ref. Sheets 57D No.65,000 No.65142
SPECIAL K.3 - M.21.

Place	Date	Hour	Summary of Events and Information	Remarks and references to Appendices
MAILLY MAILLET	23-1-17		"A" & "B" Sections (less 1 team) in the line. 2 teams of "C" Section relieved 3 teams of 9th Ch. M.G Coy in BEAUMONT HAMEL. Relief complete 4.30 pm. Weather extremely cold. Transport moved from BUS-LES-ARTOIS to BERTRANCOURT	
MAILLY MAILLET	24-1-17		1 team of "C" Section relieved 1 team of "B" at ELLIS SQUARE at 6 pm. Like relieved team also 1 team of "F" Section from REDAN withdrew to billets. MAILLY MAILLET. 2nd Lieut REED relieved 2nd Lieut HYSLOP in the line and took over command of 3 teams of "C" Section and 1 of "B". Transport at BERTRANCOURT. Detachment tiredly cold.	
MAILLY MAILLET	25-1-17		1 team of "C" Section relieved 1 team of "B" at ELLIS SQUARE at 6 pm. On relief complete the teams of "B" withdrew to billets MAILLY-MAILLET, arriving 9 pm. Transport at BERTRANCOURT. 2.0. RP to home W.K. Weather extremely cold.	

Army Form C. 2118.

WAR DIARY
INTELLIGENCE SUMMARY. 1st Machine Gun Corps

(Erase heading not required.)

Place	Date	Hour	Summary of Events and Information	Remarks and references to Appendices
MAILLY MAILLET.	26-1-17		"D" Section under 2nd Lieut O. Bentley relieved "A" Section in the line. (REDAN RIDGE) relief complete 5.45 P.M. After relief "A" Section embussed to billets MAILLY-MAILLET under 2nd Lieut M. Givens. Weather extremely cold. Transport at BERTRANCOURT.	For SHOOTS 57/D.24.C.&d SPECIAL 27TH TO NA65&2 K3 – M21 A. Bentley
MAILLY MAILLET.	27-1-17		1 team of 1st M.M.G. Battery relieved 1 team of "C" Section at Q5.c.8.8. relief complete 6.45 A.M. The team of "C" Section withdrew to position at Q.5.c.15.45 In. Burn. Work. 2 guns of "C" Section at Ellis Square, 1 at Burn-Work and 1 at BEAUMONT HAMEL. 3 guns of "D" Sections on REDAN RIDGE and 1 in LEGEND TRENCH. "A" + "B" Sections in billets MAILLY-MAILLET. Transport at BERTRANCOURT. Weather extremely cold. Owing to congestion on Tramol Railway, rations had to be fetched from tram line Unk. 1 Officer from leave Unk.	R. Bentley Lieut

Army Form C. 2118.

WAR DIARY
or
INTELLIGENCE SUMMARY. 114th Machine Gun Company

(Erase heading not required.)

Place	Date	Hour	Summary of Events and Information	Remarks and references to Appendices
			REF SHEETS 57D 40,000 20,000 M0500 SPECIAL K9 - M21	
MAILLY MAILLET	28-1-17		"B" Section relieved "C" Section on the line. 2 Guns under 2/Lt A Barrow relieved 1 Gun on LEGEND TRENCH and 1 on ELLIS SQUARE. Relief complete 6 pm. 2 Guns under Lieut. C. Birchall relieved 1 Gun on BEAUMONT HAMEL and 1 in BURN WORK. Relief complete 4.50 pm. Afterwards "C" Section on relieved to billets MAILLY MAILLET. "A" Section in billets MAILLY-MAILLET. Transport at BERTRANCOURT. Weather extremely cold.	C Birchall Lieut
MAILLY MAILLET	29-1-17		Distribution of Coy as on 28 Ct.	
MAILLY MAILLET	30-1-17		Guns moved to Points 88 (BEWA), 46, + H. Coy otherwise distributed as on 29th	

Army Form C. 2118.

WAR DIARY
INTELLIGENCE SUMMARY 10th Divl. Signal Coy.

(Erase heading not required.)

Place	Date	Hour	Summary of Events and Information Ref. Sheets. 57½ NE, NW, Special 1/10, SE 57c SW N.O.5542	Remarks and references to Appendices
MAILLY MAILLET	31-1-17		1 grm of Watling. St. moved to Bintry "D" Station under 2/Lieut O. Bentley relieved by 2/Lieut. R.L. Hyslop with "C" section. Relief complete 8pm. 1 Sec. of "A" Section went into position at Point 46. 1 Remainder of "A" Section & bullets Mailly-Maillet Transport at Bertrancourt.	January 1918

WAR DIARY
INTELLIGENCE SUMMARY

No. 13 Army Form C. 2118
1st Machine Gun Company

Ref Sheets 57d 1/40,000
Special N°64 S2H/10,000
K3 · M31

Place	Date	Hour	Summary of Events and Information	Remarks and references to Appendices
Mailly Maillet	1-2-17		"A" Section relieved gun at Ellis Square and one gun of 96th M.G. Coy. 2 teams of "B" Section withdrew from Burn-Work to billets Mailly-Maillet. 94th M.G. Coy took over position at Burn-Work. A small outbreak of fire occurred in Company Headquarters billet (K.3.d.43) at 11-15 p.m. same was extinguished by 11-35 p.m. Lieut. A. Bloomfield's kit was destroyed, little damage done to billet. Weather very cold.	Lt Bloomfield joins
Mailly Maillet	2-2-17		1 gun moved from Wolf to Point 96. 1 gun of 96th M.G. Coy was transferred to Legend. At 8 p.m. gun moved from K.2. Post 29 and thence under orders of night Company Commander 15th H.L.I. gun from Point 96 moved to Post Jogged Hare. 2/Lieut G.B.M. Reed relieved 2/Lieut M. Givens in Mouse Post and took over command of "A" Section. Weather very cold. 1 O.R. to leave U.K.	Lt Bloomfield

Army Form C. 2118.

WAR DIARY
or
INTELLIGENCE SUMMARY 14th Machine Gun Company

(Erase heading not required.)

Instructions regarding War Diaries and Intelligence Summaries are contained in F. S. Regs., Part II. and the Staff Manual respectively. Title Pages will be prepared in manuscript.

REF SHEETS 57D 1/44,000
SPECIAL Nº 6452 1/20,000

Place	Date	Hour	Summary of Events and Information	Remarks and references to Appendices
MAILLY MAILLET	3-2-19		2 Guns moved on Indicator returned to original position. Remainder of Company distributed as on the Indr. Weather very cold. I.B.R. to C.C.S. I.O.R. from Leave O.K. Transport at BERTRANCOURT.	Albrincourt ?
MAILLY MAILLET	4-2-19		"B" & "D" Sections relieved "A" & "E" in the line. "B" Section took over positions at Points 88, 3, 4, & 96. "D" Section took over positions at ENNIS SQUARE, LEGEND, and POINT 46. Relief complete 6-30 p.m. Weather extremely cold. Transport at BERTRANCOURT. I.O.R. Accidentally wounded. I.O.R. from H.Q. borne.	Albrincourt ?
MAILLY MAILLET	5-2-19		Distribution of Company as on the Indicat. 3 O.R's reinforcements joined Coy from M.G. Base Depot CAMIERS. I.O.R to C.C.S. Transport at BERTRANCOURT Weather very cold.	Albrincourt ?

WAR DIARY
or
INTELLIGENCE SUMMARY. 14th Machine Gun Company

Army Form C. 2118.

(Erase heading not required.)

Place	Date	Hour	Summary of Events and Information	Remarks and references to Appendices
MAILLY MAILLET.	11-2-17		REF SHEETS 57/D 1/40000 SPECIAL 70 6452 1/20000 2 Guns and team at CAT TUNNEL, withdrew from special position at dawn to MAILLY-MAILLET under Sergt. HARDY. 2/Lieut. A.H.D. FAIRBARNE relieved Lieut. C. BIRCHALL in the line at dawn and took over command of 1, 2, 3 & 4 positions. I.O.R. evacuated to C.C.S. Transport at BERTRANCOURT.	
MAILLY MAILLET	12-2-17		"D" Section relieved "A" Section at positions 1,2,3 & 4. "B" " " " " 5,6,7 & 8. Relief complete 8 p.m. After relief A & B Sections withdrew to billets MAILLY-MAILLET. Sections were heavily shelled on DUCKBOARDS. No casualties. I.O.R. evacuated to C.C.S. Transport at BERTRANCOURT. Weather mild.	
MAILLY MAILLET	13-2-17		Distribution of Coy as follows:- "D" Section in the line at positions 1,2,3 & 4. "B" " " " " 5,6,7 & 8. Hd Qrs, A & C Sections in billets MAILLY-MAILLET. Transport at BERTRANCOURT. Situation normal.	

Army Form C. 2118.

WAR DIARY
or
INTELLIGENCE SUMMARY. 1st Machine Gun Company

(Erase heading not required.)

Instructions regarding War Diaries and Intelligence Summaries are contained in F. S. Regs., Part II. and the Staff Manual respectively. Title pages will be prepared in manuscript.

Place	Date	Hour	Summary of Events and Information	Remarks and references to Appendices
Mailly Maillet	8-2-19		Ref Sheets 57D 1/40000 Special No 6W57 1/20000 "B" & "C" Sections relieved 13 + D in the line. "A" took over positions 1,2,3,+4. "B" took over 5,6,7,+ 8. Relief complete 4.0 P.M. After relief 13 + D proceeded to billets Mailly-Maillet. 1. OR Sergt Martin and Sergt Hardy respectively. 2/Lieut. A.L. Hyslop + 1 O.R. proceeded to leave U.K. Weather very cold. Transport at Bertrancourt.	
Mailly Maillet.	9-2-19.		1 Sub-section of "D" Section paraded under 2/Lieut. A.H.D. Fairbairns at 4.45pm to take up special position in the line, taking 5000 rds in belts per gun. 1.O.R. from No. G Course. No 60120 Pte J. Lumby accidentally wounded. 2. O.R.s reinforcements joined Coy from Big Base Depôt Camiers. Transport at Bertrancourt.	
Mailly Maillet.	10-2-19.		2 Guns at Cat Tunnel formed a barrage to assist movement of Brigade on right on to Ten Tree Alley. 14,250 rounds fired. Guns at 1+2 position also took part, firing 4,500 rounds. Wire received of ration successful. 200 prisoners taken. No 60120 Pte J. Lumby died of wounds. Transport at Bertrancourt.	

Army Form C. 2118.

WAR DIARY or INTELLIGENCE SUMMARY 14th Machine Gun Company

(Erase heading not required.)

REF SHEETS 57D 40,000 1/20,000
SPECIAL N⁰6452 1/20,000
9I3 - M31

Place	Date	Hour	Summary of Events and Information	Remarks and references to Appendices
MAILLY MAILLET	6-2-17		Distribution of Company as on the 5th inst. 2/Lieut. O. BENTLEY relieved 2/Lieut. A.H.D. FAIRBAIRNS in the line and took over command of "D" Section. Court of Enquiry held at Company Headquarters re accidental wound caused to N⁰60130. Pte. J. NEWBERT by N⁰29118 Pte. F. TOWNSEND whilst loading his revolver in billet MAILLY-MAILLET at 4.45 pm prior to his proceeding to trenches. Transport at BERTRANCOURT. 1.O.R. from leave U.K.	aldsendmillstin
MAILLY MAILLET	7-2-17		Distribution of Company as on the 6th inst. 2/Lieut. A. BARROW relieved 2/Lieut G.B.M. REED at MOUSE Post and took over command of 2 teams of "D" Section. 2/Lieut M. GIVENS + 3.O.R.s proceeded to M.G. School Camiers for course.	

Army Form C. 2118.

WAR DIARY
INTELLIGENCE SUMMARY
of 1st Machine Gun Company

(Erase heading not required.)

Instructions regarding War Diaries and Intelligence Summaries are contained in F.S. Regs., Part II. and the Staff Manual respectively. Title pages will be prepared in manuscript.

Place	Date	Hour	Summary of Events and Information	Remarks and references to Appendices
MAILLY-MAILLET	14-2-17		Company attached to 186/ Infantry Brigade. Distribution of Company as on 13th inst. Lieut. C. BIRCHALL relieved 2/Lieut. A. BARROH at MOUSE POST. 2.O.R's reinforcements joined Coy from Advanced Stores Transport Depot ABBEVILLE.	Ref Sheets 57D 1/40000 Special No 6 & 52 1/20000 113 - M91.
MAILLY-MAILLET	15-2-17		Distribution of Company as on the 14th inst.	
MAILLY-MAILLET	16-2-17		"C" Section relieved "D" Section at positions 1, 2, 3, 4. "A" " " "B" " " " 5, 6, 7, 8. Relief complete 6 P.M. After relief "B" & "D" Sections withdrew to billets MAILLY-MAILLET. 2/Lieut O. BENTLEY relieved by Lieut R.H.D. FAIRBAIRNS.	
MAILLY-MAILLET	17-2-17		Distribution of Company as follows:- "A" & "C" Sections in the Line. "B" & "D" " " and Company H.Q. in billets MAILLY-MAILLET. Transport at BERTRANCOURT.	

Army Form C. 2118.

WAR DIARY
or
INTELLIGENCE SUMMARY

14th Machine Gun Company

(Erase heading not required.)

REF SHEETS 1/40,000
SPECIAL No 6452   1/20,000
                  N3 - M21.

Place	Date	Hour	Summary of Events and Information	Remarks and references to Appendices
MAILLY MAILLET - HARPONVILLE	18.2.17		Company relieved by 20th M.G. Coy in the line. Relief complete 5-30am. On relief A + B Sections switched to billets. At 2pm Company moved to HARPONVILLE via FORCEVILLE - VARENNES arriving in billets 4-5pm and rejoined 14 Infantry Brigade	Appendices
HARPONVILLE - WARLOY	19.2.17		At 9am. Company moved to WARLOY arriving in billets at 11-15am.	Appendices
WARLOY	20.2.17		Company in billets WARLOY	Appendices
WARLOY - VILLERS - BOCAGE	21.2.17		Company moved to billets VILLERS-BOCAGE route via CONTAY - BEAUCOURT - MOLLIENS arriving 2-45pm	Appendices
VILLERS BOCAGE - ST ACHEUL	22.2.17		Company moved to billets ST ACHEUL route via PUCHVILLE and AMIENS RD arriving 3-10pm	Appendices

Army Form C. 2118.

WAR DIARY
INTELLIGENCE SUMMARY.
1st Cd. Machine Gun Coy.

(Erase heading not required.)

Instructions regarding War Diaries and Intelligence Summaries are contained in F. S. Regs., Part II and the Staff Manual respectively. Title pages will be prepared in manuscript.

REF. SHEET AMIENS 14.1/10 54

Place	Date	Hour	Summary of Events and Information	Remarks and references to Appendices
ST ACHEUL THENNES	23-2-19		Company moved to billets THENNES route via ST NICOLAS - BERTEAUCOURT arriving in billets 1-55 PM. Lieut. C. BIRCHALL 2nd Lieut. O. BENTLEY 2nd Lieut. A.H.D. FAIRBARNS (and batmen) also Sergts. F. MARTIN, N.J. BOON and N. HARDY proceeded to Std Gas 14/Inf Bde CAMON at 8.25 AM and proceeded by bus to forward area.	
THENNES - BEAUCOURT	24-2-19		Company moved to billets BEAUCOURT route via DOMART - MAISON - BLANCHE, arriving in billets 3-10 PM.	
BEAUCOURT BOIS-LONGUES (E.25t)	26-2-19		Company moved to huts.tents BOIS-LONGUES (E.25t) arriving 4-30 PM. Some difficulties were experienced in transport owing to bad condition of roads. Capt. E. WIGLEY & Lieut. A. BROOMFIELD proceeded to trenches prior to Brigade taking over the line.	
BOIS-LONGUES K.22 d 2.9	26-2-19		B, C, & D sections moved into the line and relieved French troops at 13 gun positions in sub section A, B, & C. Relief complete 2 am (2 y th) A section provided carrying parties for B, C, & D. On relief complete these parties withdrew to along with Lm. R.26.61.6 Company H.Q. K.22 d 2.9.	

Army Form C. 2118.

WAR DIARY
or
INTELLIGENCE SUMMARY. 1st Machine Gun Company

(Erase heading not required.)

Place	Date	Hour	Summary of Events and Information	Remarks and references to Appendices
			Ref: Sheets 66E.NEW 662 NW, PARTS OF 66E.S.E.	
K22d 2.9.	27-2-17		Distribution of Company as follows:— B, C, + D Sections in the line. "A" Section and Hd Qr details in dugouts La Raperie. Company Hd Qrs at K22.2.9. Transport at Bois-Longues (East). 2nd Lieut. M. Givens and 3 O.R.s rejoined Coy from M.G. Corps Camiers.	
K22d 2.9.	28-2-17		Distribution of Company as on the 27th. 2nd Lieut. A.L. Hyslop rejoined Coy from leave U.K.	

"A" Form.
MESSAGES AND SIGNALS.

Army Form C.2121
(in pads of 100).

TO 141/ Infantry Bde

Sender's Number: Q 1/2   AAA

Herewith War Diary for month of March 1917

From 141/ Machine Gun Company

Charles Buckell Lieut

Army Form C. 2118.

WAR DIARY
INTELLIGENCE SUMMARY. 14th Machine Gun Company

(Erase heading not required.)

Place	Date	Hour	Summary of Events and Information	Remarks and references to Appendices
K.22.d.2.9. K.22.t.35.40.	1-3-17		Ref. Sheets 66 N.E. & 66 N.W. 1/20,000 2nd Lieut. A. L. Hyslop rejoined his section in the line. 2nd Lieut. A. Barron went into the line prior to his section taking over position 1.2.3 & 4. Sergt E.A Jones joined Company from 20 th M.G.Coy and took over duties of C.Q.M.S.	(Rowles Birchall Lieut)
K.22.t.35.40.	2-3-17		"A" Section under 2nd Lieut M. Givens relieved "B" Section in the right sector of the line. Relief complete. 8 p.m. On relief "B" Section under Lieut. C. Birchall withdrew to dug-outs at LA RAPERIE and K.22.t.35.40. respectively. Company transport moved to lines at FRESNOY EN CHAUSSEE.	(Rowles Birchall Lieut)
K.22.t.35.40.	3-3-17		"A" Section at position 1, 2, 3 & 4. "C" " " " 5, 6, 7 & 8. "D" " " " 9, 10, 11 & 12. "B" " in dug-outs LA RAPERIE. Transport at FRESNOY EN CHAUSSEE.	(Rowles Birchall Lieut)

Army Form C. 2118.

WAR DIARY
or
INTELLIGENCE SUMMARY.

14th Machine Gun Coy

(Erase heading not required.)

Place	Date	Hour	Summary of Events and Information	Remarks and references to Appendices
K22 b 35.40	4-3-17		Company distributed as on the 3rd	Ref sheets 57E N.E & 57D N.W. (Rules Budgell) Kiwi 1/22,000
K22 b 35.40	5-3-17		Company distributed as on the 4th	(Rules Budgell) Kiwi
K22 b 35.40	6-3-17		Company distributed as on the 5th	(Rules Budgell) Kiwi
			A Field General Court Martial assembled at Company Headquarters for trial of:-	
			16461 Sergt. EWEN. J.)	
			15231 " LEONARD. P.) 14th Machine Gun Coy	
			16248 Corpl PARKER. F.) adjt	
			No 16923 Corpl C. DARLING & 16255 L/Cpl W. HAWKE	
			Proceeded to Machine Gun Corps Base Depot CAMIERS	
			to proceed to ENGLAND. Authority A.G. No 6864 d/ 23-10-16.	
K22 b 35.40	7-3-17		Company distributed as on the 6th inst	(Rules Budgell) Kiwi
K22 b 35.40	8-3-17		Company distributed as on the 7th inst.	(Rules Budgell) Kiwi
K22 b 35.40 BEAUCOURT	9-3-17		Company Headquarters moved to billets BEAUCOURT arriving at 5-15 p.m. A.C. & D. Sections relieved in dug-outs Right, Centre & Left, respectively by three sections of 96th Machine Gun Coy. Relief complete 8-40 p.m On relief, sections under 2nd Lieuts. M. GIVENS. A.L. HYSLOP, & O. BENTLEY withdrew to billets BEAUCOURT. arriving 10-30 p.m.	(Rules Budgell) Kiwi

Army Form C. 2118.

WAR DIARY

INTELLIGENCE SUMMARY 1st Ch Machine Gun Coy

(Erase heading not required.)

Instructions regarding War Diaries and Intelligence Summaries are contained in F. S. Regs., Part II. and the Staff Manual respectively. Title Pages will be prepared in manuscript.

Place	Date	Hour	Summary of Events and Information	Remarks and references to Appendices
BEAUCOURT	10-3-17		Company in billets cleaning guns and gun equipment.	Ref Sheets AMIENS 14 1/100000 (Charles Buckell Lieut)
BEAUCOURT	11-3-17		Company in billets training.	(Charles Buckell Lieut)
BEAUCOURT	12-3-17		Company in billets training 8.30AM to 12.30PM Company detailed baths at BEAUCOURT.	(Charles Buckell Lieut)
BEAUCOURT	13-3-17		Company in billets training	(Charles Buckell Lieut)
BEAUCOURT	14-3-17		2nd Lt. A.L. HYSLOP, 2nd Lt. M.GIVENS, 9.8. O.R's proceeded to line for instruction in sector prior to Company taking over same from 94th M.G. Coy	Ref Sheet 66E 1/40000 (Charles Buckell Lieut)
Eg. q. 5	15-3-17		Company relieved 94th M.G. Coy in the line in positions in front of FOCQUESCOURT. Relief complete 8.30 P.M.	(Charles Buckell Lieut)

Army Form C. 2118.

WAR DIARY
of
INTELLIGENCE SUMMARY. 101/ Machine Gun Coy

(Erase heading not required.)

Instructions regarding War Diaries and Intelligence Summaries are contained in F.S. Regs., Part II. and the Staff Manual respectively. Title pages will be prepared in manuscript.

Place	Date	Hour	Summary of Events and Information	Remarks and references to Appendices
			Ref Sheet 66 E 1/40,000	
E.39.c.5	16-3-17		Company in the line. Lieut. A. BLOOMFIELD proceeded to join 12/Machine Gun Coy (Appointed C.O.)	(Charles Birchall) Lieut
E.39.c.5	17-3-17		Withdrawal of the enemy. C & D Sections attached to 15th L.F. and 2nd Manchesters respectively, moved forward into enemy third line. A + B Sections in reserve in our own line. Company H.Q. established in our reserve line. Weather fine. Casualties Nil.	(Charles Birchall) Lieut
LIANCOURT	18-3-17		C & D Sections attached to 15th H.L.I and 2nd Manchesters respectively moved forward and established line on night 18/19 from BOIS-D-HERLY to ETALON. A + B Sections in reserve and Company H.Q. moved via FOUQUESCOURT- FRANSART- HATTENCOURT to LIANCOURT arriving 11 P.M. Remarks. Weather fine. Little difficulty experienced in moving transport. Casualties Nil.	(Charles Birchall) Lieut

Army Form C. 2118.

WAR DIARY
or of
INTELLIGENCE SUMMARY. 1st Machine Gun Coy.
(Erase heading not required.)

Instructions regarding War Diaries and Intelligence Summaries are contained in F. S. Regs., Part II. and the Staff Manual respectively. Title pages will be prepared in manuscript.

Place	Date	Hour	Summary of Events and Information	Remarks and references to Appendices
LIANCOURT – NESLE – MESNIL ST NICAISE	19-3-17		On morning of 19th C & D Sections were relieved by A & B Sections who were attacked to 5/6 S.F. Shots & 1st Dorsets respectively and moved forward and established a line of advance from VOYENNES to ROUY-LE-PETIT. Company H.Q. moved forward leaving LIANCOURT at 10-30 am and joined C & D Section at LICOURNE'S WOOD and moved via HERLY to NESLE arriving 11-55 am. At 3-1-45 pm H. Qrs. C & D Sections moved to MESNIL-ST-NICAISE arriving at 4-50 pm. Remarks. Weather fine. Casualties Nil.	Ref Sheet 66d N.W. 1/20,000 Charles Bucknell Lieut
MESNIL ST NICAISE.	20-3-17		Two forward sections were moved forward to vicinity of MATIGNY in line of advance. H. Qrs C & D Sections and transport in billets MESNIL ST NICAISE. Remarks. Weather wet & cold. Casualties Nil.	Charles Bucknell Lieut
MESNIL ST NICAISE – VOYENNES	21-3-17		H. Qrs. & C & D Sections in reserve moved forward at 11-30 am via ROUY-LE-GRAND to VOYENNES arriving at 12-15 pm. At 1-30 pm C Section went forward in support to A & B Sections in line of advance. Remarks. Weather wet & cold. Casualties Nil.	Charles Bucknell Lieut

Army Form C. 2118.

WAR DIARY
INTELLIGENCE SUMMARY. 1/4/ Hampshire Regt

(Erase heading not required.)

Place	Date	Hour	Summary of Events and Information	Remarks and references to Appendices
VOYENNES	22-3-17		A, B & C Sections in line of resistance MATIGNY. D Section at VOYENNES in reserve. 2 guns of this section being mounted in village for defence against hostile aircraft. Remarks, Weather cold & showery. Casualties Nil.	Ref Sheet ST QUENTIN 15 1/100 000 [signed] Charles Buchell Lieut
VOYENNES	23-3-17		Distribution of Lewis guns on the 22nd int. At 4.30 a.m. 10 MG guns in defence against aircraft fired 150 rounds at hostile aeroplane which disappeared in a S Easterly direction. H QR reinforcements found by from H.Q. Base Depot CAMIERS. Weather fine. Casualties Nil.	[signed] Charles Buchell Lieut
VOYENNES	24-3-17		"A" Section withdrew from line of resistance to held in reserve at VOYENNES arriving at 1-15 p.m. Distribution of Company as follows:- B & C Sections in line of resistance MATIGNY H. Qrs A & D Sections and Transport at VOYENNES. Summer Time adopted by British Armies in France. 11 P.M. became 12 midnight. Weather fine. Casualties Nil.	[signed] Charles Buchell Lieut

[signed] Charles Buchell Lieut |

Army Form C. 2118.

WAR DIARY
of
INTELLIGENCE SUMMARY. 14/ Machine Gun Coy

(Erase heading not required.)

Instructions regarding War Diaries and Intelligence Summaries are contained in F. S. Regs., Part II. and the Staff Manual respectively. Title pages will be prepared in manuscript.

Place	Date	Hour	Summary of Events and Information	Remarks and references to Appendices
VOYENNES	25.3.17		D. Section relieved "B" Section in line of resistance. Relief complete 4 P.M. after relief complete "B" Section withdrew to billets vacated by "D" Section at VOYENNES arriving 4.50 PM. Weather fine. Gauntlets Nil.	Ref. Sheets 66d & 62d 1/40.000 Charles Birchall Lieut
VOYENNES	26.3.17		Distribution of Coy as on the 25th. Weather fine. Gauntlets Nil.	Charles Birchall Lieut
VOYENNES	27.3.17		Distribution of Coy as on the 26th. Weather cold & showery. Gauntlets Nil.	Charles Birchall Lieut
VOYENNES — BEAUVOIS	28.3.17	5.30 pm	At 5.30 pm. Company (less C & D Section) left VOYENNES and marched to BEAUVOIS arriving 8.40 PM. On night 28/29 d 14/ Infantry Bde took up General Line E.6.c CENTRAL - E.6.a - W.30.c - W.30.a - W.29.b — and at W.23.a - W.17.c - W.16.d sick outposts on the line X.20 d 6.2. - X.13 & 3.9. Company distributed as follows:- D. Section attached to 2/Manchesters, A + B Section in the General Line, C Section in BEAUVOIS in Reserve. Coy HQrs BEAUVOIS. Transport at VGNY. Weather cold & showery. Very poor billets. Gauntlets Nil.	Charles Birchall Lieut

WAR DIARY
INTELLIGENCE SUMMARY

14/ Machine Gun Coy

Army Form C. 2118.

Place	Date	Hour	Summary of Events and Information	Remarks and references to Appendices
BEAUVOIS	29-3-17		Distribution of Coy as on the night of 28/29th. Section of 219 M.G. Coy attached for instruction. Weather cold & wet. Gonnelieu N.w.	Ref. Sheets 66ᶜ & 66ˢ 1/40,000 Charles Buckhshiew
BEAUVOIS	30-3-17		Section of 219th M.G. Coy attached for instruction relieved 2 teams of A & B Sections respectively. On relief teams of A & B Sections withdrew to billets BEAUVOIS. Weather cold & showery. Gonnelieu N.w.	Charles Buckhshiew
BEAUVOIS	31-3-17		At 5-30 A.M. D. Section withdrew from line to billets BEAUVOIS. At 5-30 P.M. "C" Section took up position vacated by D Section. Weather cold & showery.	Charles Buckhshiew

Charles Buckhshiew
for O.C. 14. M.G. Coy.

WAR DIARY / INTELLIGENCE SUMMARY

Army Form C. 2118.

Vol 15

114th Machine Gun Company

Ref. Sheet 62. B.3. at 1/20.000.

Place	Date	Hour	Summary of Events and Information	Remarks and references to Appendices
BEAUVOIS CHATEAU-DE POMMERY	1.4.17		Company (less two sections) and one section of 219th M.G. Company proceeded to fresh quarters 96th Infantry Brigade. During the afternoon three sections with an extra one from 219th Company making it sections were placed under my command and proceeded through ROUPY and took up positions in 73d's 92. At 3 p.m. intense fire was brought to bear on L'EPINE-DE-BALLON and ridge to left which was occupied by the enemy and Machine Guns. The operations was so successful that enemy machine guns had to evacuate many advanced positions, 60,000 rounds were fired. Two sections at M.G. positions in defence of BEAUVOIS were relieved by two sections of 104th M.G. Company. Relief complete 4 p.m. At 5.30 p.m. Company (less two sections) marched to F.G.2 CHATEAU-DE-POMMERY leaving 6.30a at 6.35 p.m., arriving at 9.27 p.m. At 11 p.m. two sections moved off with 3d Infantry Brigade. Company Headquarters bivouaced at CHATEAU-DE-POMMERY. Transport (two gun limbers at Headquarters) moved to VAUX. Weather fine. Casualties Nil.	S.S.5

2353 Wt. W2544/1454 700,000 5/15 D. D. & L. A.D.S.S. (Forms/C. 2118.

Army Form C. 2118.

WAR DIARY
or
INTELLIGENCE SUMMARY.
(Erase heading not required.)

14th Cheshire Regt. Company Ref. Sheet 62.S.W. 1/20,000.

Place	Date	Hour	Summary of Events and Information	Remarks and references to Appendices
REAR H.QRS. CHATEAU DE POMMERY FORWARD H.QRS. SAVY	24.4.17		At 5.0 a.m. 14th Infantry Brigade attacked on villages of "P". A.B.C. Sections attached to 1st Dorsets, 2nd Manchesters & 15th Highland L.I. respectively. "D" section kept in position on extreme right flank putting up intense fire on enemy right flank. In the early morning themselves Lts. 2nd Lieut. A.L. HYSLOP and No.11067 Sergt. N.J. BOON went forward to make a reconnaissance, but did not return, they must have walked into the enemy lines and taken prisoners. No.16452 Sergt. F. FLATTLEY took over command of the section and led same very ably during the operations. "A" section with 1st Dorsets took up their position round the village of HORNON paying special attention to the left flank and Bois HORNON. 2nd Lieut. M. Givens wounded in leg at about 4.30 p.m. by M.G. fire. "B" section with 2nd Manchesters showed great tenacity and skill in handling their guns. No.62248 Private F. PARKER got his gun quickly into action against the enemy with such good results that they steamed and ran from SERENCY. No.16525 Sgt. T. PORTER engaged an enemy field Battery at short range, the enemy gunners being unable to man	L.S.N.

Army Form C. 2118.

WAR DIARY
or
INTELLIGENCE SUMMARY.
(Erase heading not required.)

of 14th Machine Gun Company

Ref Sheet 62 O.S.W. 1/20,000

Place	Date	Hour	Summary of Events and Information	Remarks and references to Appendices
	2nd Contd		Their guns which greatly assisted the 15th Bn. Y.L.I. on their right. Suggery in this gun pit in action until eventually blown up by an enemy shell. Later in the morning Capt. J.N. IRONSIDE sended heavy enemy shell fire dispersed a large body of the enemy massing near the BOIS-DE-ROSES. "C" Section with the 15th Bn. H.L.I. dug in positions and defended the Ridge from S.E. of FRANCILLY - SERENCY and PT. 138. From time to time these guns dispersed bodies of the enemy with good results. "D" Section after three operations in out extreme right flank in the early hours proceeded to SAVY via ROUPY and remained in Brigade Reserve. Weather very stormy and cold. Casualties:- 2nd Lieut. M. GIVENS Wounded. " A.L. HYSLOP Missing. 1. O.R. Killed. 1. O.R. Missing. 5. O.R° Wounded.	

Army Form C. 2118.

WAR DIARY
—or—
INTELLIGENCE SUMMARY.
(Erase heading not required.)

of 14th Machine Gun Company. Ref. Sheet 62.S.W.1/20,000

Place	Date	Hour	Summary of Events and Information	Remarks and references to Appendices
REGR HD.QRS CHATEAU-DE POMMERY FORWARD HD QRS SAVY.	3.4.17		A, B & C Sections supported the Infantry on the line SAVY 138 FRANCILLY - SELENCY & HOLNON under heavy enemy shell and machine gun fire. Casualties NIL. Weather fine.	BM
″	4.4.17		The 1st Infantry Brigade advanced its left flank from SELENCY N. of Bois M.93 with left of HOLNON + FRESNOY to 'PETIT' ROAD nr Bois 17. 32 d. 'D' Section at SAVY were ordered to support the 1st DORSETS with "A" Section. In this advance all guns were in position and dug in before daylight April 5th. Weather Snowstorms Casualties 1.O.R. Wounded.	BM
″	5.4.17		Guns of A & D Sections fired 4,000 rounds into FAYET and 3,000 rounds on FRESNOY-LE-PETIT. Weather fine. Casualties 1.O.R. Wounded.	BM

WAR DIARY
INTELLIGENCE SUMMARY.
(Erase heading not required.)

Army Form C. 2118.

of 1th S. Machine Gun Company

Map Sheet. 62 B S.W. 1/20,000
ST. QUENTIN 18/1/1/100,000

Place	Date	Hour	Summary of Events and Information	Remarks and references to Appendices
REAR H.QRS CHATEAU DE POMMERY	6.4.17		Guns of A Coy taking gun transports into turrets of fire to bear on FAYET, FRESNOY-LE-PETIT, 8,000 rounds being fired. Weather wet. Casualties Nil.	
FORWARD H.QRS SAVY				
SAVY 7.4.17 FORESTE			Company was relieved by 99th Machine Gun Company, whereupon Company proceeded to Billets at FORESTE. Relief complete 1.30 p.m. 10 O.R.s reinforcements joined Company from M.G. BASE DEPOT CAMIERS. Weather fine. Casualties Nil.	
FORESTE 8.4.17			Company in billets cleaning guns and equipment etc. Weather fine. Casualties Nil.	

Army Form C. 2118.

WAR DIARY
or
INTELLIGENCE SUMMARY.
(Erase heading not required.)

Instructions regarding War Diaries and Intelligence Summaries are contained in F. S. Regs., Part II. and the Staff Manual respectively. Title pages will be prepared in manuscript.

of 14th Machine Gun Company

Army Sheet 57 Qu.se NW16. 1/100,000

Place	Date	Hour	Summary of Events and Information	Remarks and references to Appendices
FORESTE	9.4.17		Company in billets cleaning equipment etc. Weather showery. Casualties NIL.	
FORESTE	10.4.17		Company in billets training. Weather showery. Casualties NIL.	
FORESTE	11.4.17		Company in readiness to move forward at half an hours notice. Weather showery. Casualties Nil. Joined Company from M.G. Base Depot CAMIERS. Lieut. G. R. DAVIDSON 2/Lieut. F. FARMBROUGH	

Army Form C. 2118.

WAR DIARY
or
INTELLIGENCE SUMMARY.
(Erase heading not required.)

Instructions regarding War Diaries and Intelligence Summaries are contained in F. S. Regs., Part II. and the Staff Manual respectively. Title pages will be prepared in manuscript.

of 114 Machine Gun Company

Ref Sheet 62.S.W. 1/20,000

Place	Date	Hour	Summary of Events and Information	Remarks and references to Appendices
FORWARD Hd Qrs. SAVY. REAR Hd. Qrs. GERMAINE.	12.4.17		Company relieved 96th M.G. Company. A.C&D. Sections in the line and 'B' Section in reserve. Railway Cutting BOIS-DES-SAVY. Forward Headquarters were established in village of SAVY. Rear Headquarters and Transport at GERMAINE. Weather showery. Casualties Nil.	52A
	13.4.17	1.45am to 5.45am	16 Guns opened fire on enemy line S.24a.0.0. to S.18.d.8.2. in support of the French in an attack on our right on ST. QUENTIN. 50,000 rounds were fired.	
		6 a.m.	1st DORSETS moved forward and took up a forward line of posts running from S.23d to BOIS-DES-ROSES in S.10a. 'B' Section attached to them placing one gun in S.P.S.23a.1.6. One gun in S.17.c.6.5. and two guns in BOIS-DES-ROSES S/15.2.9.	
		12.noon.	A&B Sections placed in position about S.22 CENTRAL to support	53A

2353 Wt. W3544/4454 700,000 5/15 D. D. & L. A.D.S.S./Forms/C. 2118.

Army Form C. 2118.

WAR DIARY
INTELLIGENCE SUMMARY.
(Erase heading not required.)

Instructions regarding War Diaries and Intelligence Summaries are contained in F.S. Regs., Part II. and the Staff Manual respectively. Title pages will be prepared in manuscript.

114 Machine Gun Company

Ref Sheet 62 c S.W. 1/20,000

Place	Date	Hour	Summary of Events and Information	Remarks and references to Appendices
	13.4.17 Contd	12. noon	second French attack on ST. QUENTIN	
		6 p.m.	A.B. Sections brought fire to bear on enemy line in ROCOURT	
		6.15 p.m.	SALIENT to support French attack, 10,000 rounds being fired	
		9.0 p.m.	"C" Section moved from PETIT BOIS S.26.d to BOIS des ROSES and attached 1st DORSETS	
			Weather Wet.	
			Casualties: 4 O.R's Wounded.	63 N
SQVY.	14.4.17		Two Sections (two Guns each) in BOIS-DES-ROSES co-operated with 94th Infantry Bde. attack on FAYET. Fire being brought to bear on enemy position in sunken road. S.12.a. & b. M.G. emplacement S.12.c.1.6. and HINDENBURG LINE S.12.d., 19000 rounds being fired.	
		9 a.m.	"G" Section in BOIS-DES-ROSES co-operated with 1st DORSETS in attack on SEPY FARM. Overhead fire was brought to bear on the FARM by two guns in BOIS. DES. ROSES. Two guns went forward and got into position in Sunken Road S.12.D.8.8. from where intense fire was brought	63 N

WAR DIARY
INTELLIGENCE SUMMARY.

(Erase heading not required.)

Army Form C. 2118.

114th Machine Gun Company
Ref. Sheet 62.c.S.W.1/20,000

Place	Date	Hour	Summary of Events and Information	Remarks and references to Appendices
	14.4.17 Contd.		to bear on the FARM the enemy being decimated. Infantry went forward and took FARM without opposition and many dead Germans were found dead riddled with machine gun bullets. On FARM being taken 2 guns in Sunken Road pushed forward to EAST of SEPT FARM. These two guns of "C" Section were relieved at 109.m. by "B" Section, their guns being placed at S.12.a.9.4., S.12.c.0.6., S.6.d.9.3. & S.6.a.9.6. On relieving the two guns of "C" Section withdrew to position in QUARRY W. of R./138. Weather: fine. Casualties: 1 O.R. killed. 5 O.R's (Wounded). Lieut S.S. WORTH (184 M.G.Coy) joined Company appointed 2nd in Command.	66H
ST. QUENTIN	15.4.17	10.p.m	Enemy shelled out line heavily during the day. In afternoon 1 gun of "C" Section was put out of action by enemy shell fire from SEPT FARM. "A" Section in QUARRY relieved "B" Section in SEPT FARM who in	68H

Army Form C. 2118.

WAR DIARY
or
INTELLIGENCE SUMMARY.
(Erase heading not required.)

of 116 Machine Gun Company

Place	Date	Hour	Summary of Events and Information	Remarks and references to Appendices
	15.4.17 Contd		relief proceeded to QUARRY. A & B Sections fired on enemy positions in ST. QUENTIN 5,000 rounds. Casualties Nil.	Ref Sheet 62 c N.W. 1/20,000
SAVY	16.4.17		Heavy enemy shelling along whole front during the day and M.G. fired 5,060 rounds on enemy in ST. QUENTIN. At dusk withdrew 2 guns of "B" Section and 1 of "C" Section from BOIS-DES-ROSES & MONT to QUARRY. Casualties:- 3. O.R. Killed. 4. O.R. Wounded.	
SAVY	17.4.17	9.A.M.	Continuous enemy shelling especially CEPY FARM & BOIS-DES-ROSES. During morning 16 M.G. positions were sighted in BROWN LINE with Brigade Major. S9.a.1 b. S17.b.3.4. "B" Section relieved 2 guns of "D" Section at S28.a.1.6 / S17.d.2.1. and	

Army Form C. 2118.

WAR DIARY
or
INTELLIGENCE SUMMARY.
(Erase heading not required.)

Instructions regarding War Diaries and Intelligence Summaries are contained in F. S. Regs., Part II. and the Staff Manual respectively. Title pages will be prepared in manuscript.

Ref/Sheet. 62 B.S.W. 1/20.000

Place	Date	Hour	Summary of Events and Information	Remarks and references to Appendices
	17.4.17 Cont.d		2 guns of "C" Section at Bois-des-Roses who on relief proceeded to QUARRY. Casualties Nil.	
SAVY	18.4.17		During the day C.V.D. sections made M.G. emplacements in BROWN LINE. Enemy heavily shelled SAVY with 15 c.m. from 4 p.m. to 5 p.m. Must shelling of our front line by the enemy. Casualties Nil.	
SAVY	19.4.17	2 a.m. 6.30 p.m. 3 p.m. to 5 p.m. 7 p.m.	Intense enemy fire on CEPY FARM; one team was buried but no casualties. SAVY was heavily shelled by enemy 15 cm. Withdrew from SEPY FARM 1 gun being placed on 110 contour S.6.d. to cover all enemy approaches to farm. Casualties Nil. C.O.R.s reinforcements joined Company from M.G. Base Depot CAMIERS.	

Army Form C. 2118.

WAR DIARY
or
INTELLIGENCE SUMMARY.

(Erase heading not required.)

Of 14th Machine Gun Company

Ref Sheet. ST. QUENTIN 1st 1/100,000

Place	Date	Hour	Summary of Events and Information	Remarks and references to Appendices
SAVY	20.4.17	8.0pm to 9.0pm	In the morning Lieut F. Geo. & transport proceeded to QUIVIERES and took over billets from 182nd Machine Gun Company. Our M.G. fired at ST. QUENTIN 6000 rounds. Weather fine. Casualties. 1. O.R. Wounded. 1. O.R. " (accidental)	
SAVY QUIVIERES	21.4.17		Company relieved by 182nd M.G. Company at 4.0 a.m. whereupon they proceeded to billets at QUIVIERES. Casualties Nil.	
QUIVIERES	22.4.17		Company in billets resting. 6. O.R's joined Company from M.G. Base Depôt Camiers	

Army Form C. 2118.

WAR DIARY
INTELLIGENCE SUMMARY.
(Erase heading not required.)

of 14th Machine Gun Company

Place	Date	Hour	Summary of Events and Information	Remarks and references to Appendices
			Ref. Sheet ST.QUENTIN 18 1/100,000	
QUIVIERES	23.4.17		Company in billets training.	
QUIVIERES	24.4.17		Company in billets training.	
QUIVIERES	25.4.17		Company in billets training. Anti-gas appliances of Company inspected by Brigade Gas N.C.O. Arms of Company inspected by Brigade Armourer Sergeant.	
QUIVIERES	26.4.17		Company in billets training.	
QUIVIERES	27.4.17		Inspection of 14th Infantry Bde by G.O.C. at 10 a.m. on Parade Ground (E.13.B.4.4) Weather fine.	
QUIVIERES	28.4.17		Company in billets training. Weather fine.	

Army Form C. 2118.

WAR DIARY
or
INTELLIGENCE SUMMARY.

(Erase heading not required.)

14th Machine Gun Company.

Ref. Sheet ST. QUENTIN 1st 1/100,000.

Place	Date	Hour	Summary of Events and Information	Remarks and references to Appendices
QUIVIERS	29.4.17		Company in billets training. Weather fine. 2nd Lieut. E.H. DAVIES joined Company from M.G. Base Depot, CAMIERS	A/1
QUIVIERS	30.4.17		14th Infantry Bde. inspected by G.O.C. 32nd Division at 11.30 a.m. on parade ground N. of DOVILLY. Weather fine.	A/2

S.D. Smith Capt.
for O.C. 14th Machine Gun Company.

WAR DIARY of INTELLIGENCE SUMMARY.

(Erase heading not required.)

14 M.G. Coy Army Form C. 2118.

No. 14 MACHINE GUN COMPANY.

Ref Sheet 66D 1/40,000

Place	Date	Hour	Summary of Events and Information	Remarks and references to Appendices
QUIVIERES.	1.5.17		Company in billets training.	
QUIVIERES.	2.5.17	11. O.R.s	Reinforcements joined Company from M.G.C. Base Depot CAMIERS. Company in billets training.	
		9.30 a.m.	Company with 14th Infantry Brigade were inspected by II Corps Commander on Parade Ground N. of DOUILLY. 2nd Lieut. J.C. NUTHALL joined Company from M.G.C. Base Depot CAMIERS.	
QUIVIERES.	3.5.17		Company in billets training: Routine as follows:-	
		8.15 a.m. to 12.45 p.m.	"A" & "B" Sections took part in "Practice Attack" with the 2nd Bn. MANCHESTER Regt. and 1st Bn. DORSET Regt. respectively. "C" & "D" Sections training under Section Officers.	
QUIVIERES.	4.5.17		Company in billets training. Routine as follows:-	
		7.45 a.m. to 11 a.m.	"A", "B" & "D" Sections general training.	
		11 a.m. to 2 p.m.	"C" Section co-operated with 5/6 Bn. ROYAL SCOTS in a "Practice Attack".	
		2.45 p.m. to 5 p.m.	"D" Section co-operated with 15 Bn. HIGHLAND LIGHT INFANTRY.	

WAR DIARY
of 3B
INTELLIGENCE SUMMARY.
(Erase heading not required.)

Army Form C. 2118.

NO. 14 MACHINE GUN COMPANY.

Ref Sheet 66D 1/40,000

Place	Date	Hour	Summary of Events and Information	Remarks and references to Appendices
QUIVIERES.	5.5.17		Company in billets training. Concert held by Company at Royal Flying Corps Concert Hall Guizancourt at 6.p.m.	
QUIVIERES.	6.5.17		Company in billets training. Divine Services attended by the different denominations of the Company.	
QUIVIERES.	7.5.17		Company in billets training.	
QUIVIERES.	8.5.17		Company in billets: little training done owing to wet weather.	
QUIVIERES.	9.5.17	8 A.M. 8.30 A.M. 9.15 A.M. to 12.45 P.M.	Company in billets training; Routine as follows:— Inspection. Physical training. Company co-operated with 2nd Bn. Manchester Regt in a Practice Trench to Trench Attack. 2.30 p.m. Recreation.	

Army Form C. 2118.

WAR DIARY
of
INTELLIGENCE SUMMARY.

No. 14 MACHINE GUN COMPANY.

(Erase heading not required.)

Ref Sheet 66D 1/40000

Place	Date	Hour	Summary of Events and Information	Remarks and references to Appendices
QUIVIERES	10.5.17		Company in billets training. Routine as follows:-	
		7.30 a.m. to 7.45 a.m.	Inspection.	
		8.0 a.m. to 8.30 a.m.	Physical Training.	
		8.30 a.m. to 9.30 a.m.	Cleaning guns etc.	
		10.0 a.m. to 12.45 p.m.	Skeleton trench digging	
QUIVIERES	11.5.17		Company in billets training.	
		7.30 a.m. to 7.45 a.m.	Inspection.	
		7.45 a.m. to 8.15 a.m.	Physical Training.	
		8.30 a.m. to 9.30 a.m.	Cleaning guns etc.	
		9.30 a.m. to 12.45 p.m.	Company co-operated with the 2nd Bn. Manchester Regt. in a Trench to Trench Attack.	
QUIVIERES	12.5.17		Company in billets training.	
		7.30 a.m. to 7.45 a.m.	Inspection.	

Army Form C. 2118.

WAR DIARY
of
INTELLIGENCE SUMMARY.
(Erase heading not required.)

No. 14 MACHINE GUN COMPANY.

Instructions regarding War Diaries and Intelligence Summaries are contained in F. S. Regs., Part II. and the Staff Manual respectively. Title pages will be prepared in manuscript.

Place	Date	Hour	Summary of Events and Information	Remarks and references to Appendices
QUIVIERES	12.5.17 CONTD	7.45 A.M. to 8.15 A.M. 8.30 A.M. to 12.30 P.M.	Physical training. Selecting positions for Machine Guns & digging emplacements.	Ref Sheet 66 D 1/40000
QUIVIERES	13.5.17		Company attended Divine Services.	
QUIVIERES	14.5.17	7.0 A.M. to 1.0 P.M.	Company took part in a Brigade Practice Attack.	
QUIVIERES	15.5.17	5 A.M.	Company moved in accordance with 14/Inf Bde Operation Order No 130 to OFFOY route via UGNY - DOUILLY & TOULLE arriving at 7.45 A.M.	
OFFOY				
OFFOY	16.5.17	5 - 9 A.M	Company moved to LIANCOURT route via VOYENNES - NESLE - CURCHY arriving at 10-15 A.M.	
LIANCOURT				
LIANCOURT	17.5.17	6 A.M	Company moved to WARVILLERS, route via FRANSART - FOUQUESCOURT - ROUVROY arriving 9 A.M.	Sheet 66 E 1/40000
WARVILLERS				

Army Form C. 2118.

WAR DIARY
of
INTELLIGENCE SUMMARY.
(Erase heading not required.)

No. 14 MACHINE GUN COMPANY.

Instructions regarding War Diaries and Intelligence Summaries are contained in F.S. Regs., Part II. and the Staff Manual respectively. Title pages will be prepared in manuscript.

Place	Date	Hour	Summary of Events and Information	Remarks and references to Appendices
			Ref Sheet 66E 1/40,000	
WARVILLERS	18-5-17			
LE QUESNEL			Company moved to LE QUESNEL, via BEAUFORT arriving 9-15 AM	
LE QUESNEL	19-5-17		Company in billets cleaning guns, equipment etc	
LE QUESNEL	20-5-17		Company attended Divine Services.	
LE QUESNEL	21-5-17	7-45 AM to 12-45 PM	Company in fields training. "A" & "B" Section on Range (Ball firing)	
		10-15 AM to 12-30 PM	"C" Section co-operated with 5/6th R. Scots in Practice attack.	
			"D" Section co-operated with 2nd Bn MANCHESTER REGT. in Practice attack.	
LE QUESNEL	22-5-17	7-45 AM to 12-45 PM	"C" & "D" Sections on Range.	
		9-45 AM to 12-30 PM	"A" Section co-operated with 1st Bn DORSET REGT. in practice attack over trenches.	
			"B" Section co-operated with 15th Bn H.L.I. in Practice attack.	
LE QUESNEL	23-5-17	8 AM to 12 noon	Company took part in Brigade Practice attack which took place on the German system of trenches at FOUQUESCOURT. Zero time being 10-0 AM.	

Army Form C. 2118.

WAR DIARY
of
INTELLIGENCE SUMMARY 4th Machine Gun Coy.

(Erase heading not required.)

Ref Sheet 66E 1/40,000

Place	Date	Hour	Summary of Events and Information	Remarks and references to Appendices
LE QUESNEL	24-5-17	7.45am to 11-30pm 2 PM	"A, B, C, + D Sections on Range (Ball firing). Company were bathed and each man received a clean change of underclothing at Bath House BEAUCOURT.	
LE QUESNEL	25-5-17	8am to 12 noon	Company took part in Brigade Practice Attack as on the 23rd.	
LE QUESNEL	26-5-17	8am to 12 noon	Company took part in Brigade Practice Attack as on the 25th, which was observed by the Army Staff.	
LE QUESNEL	27-5-17		Company attended Divine Service. During the afternoon Brigade Sports were held in the vicinity of LE-QUESNEL and a very enjoyable afternoon was spent.	
LE QUESNEL	28-5-17		This day was recognised as a holiday and a proportion of the Company were granted leave to AMIENS.	

WAR DIARY
INTELLIGENCE SUMMARY

Instructions regarding War Diaries and Intelligence Summaries are contained in F.S. Regs., Part II. and the Staff Manual respectively. Title pages will be prepared in manuscript.

Army Form C. 2118.

14/ Machine Gun Coy.

(Erase heading not required.)

Place	Date	Hour	Summary of Events and Information	Remarks and references to Appendices
			Ref Sheet 66E 1/40,000	
LE QUESNEL	29-5-17	7.30AM to 7-45AM	Company in billets training.	
		7.45AM to 8.15 AM	Inspection by Section Officers	
		8-15AM to 9-30AM	Physical Training	
		9-30AM to 11-0 AM	Cleaning Guns etc	
		11-0 AM to 12.45 PM	Cleaning Belts and Ammunition. Packing Limbers prior to move.	
			Sheet 62D 1/40,000 66E 1/40,000	
LE QUESNEL MARCELCAVE	30-5-17	6.30 AM	Company moved to MARCELCAVE route via MAISON-BLANCHE Cross Roads D19, C13, DEMUIN. AUBERCOURT arriving at 10-45PM. 10.OR reinforcements joined Coy from M.G.Base Depot.	
MARCELCAVE	31-5-17	8-0AM to 8-16 AM	Company in billets training.	
		8-15AM to 9.15AM	Inspection by Section Officers	
		9.30 AM to 12.45 PM	Close Order Drill and Rifle Exercises. Training under Section Officers	
		11-0 PM	Transport paraded for purpose of entraining at 11-30 PM.	

E.B. Wyatt Lieut
for O.C. 14/M.G.Coy

"A" Form.
MESSAGES AND SIGNALS.

Army Form C.2121
(in pads of 100).
No. of Message ....

Prefix .... Code .... m.	Words	Charge	This message is on a/c of:	Recd. at .... m.
Office of Origin and Service Instructions.	Sent		.... Service.	Date ....
	At .... m.			From ....
	To			
	By		(Signature of "Franking Officer.")	By ....

TO { 14th Infantry Bde.

| Sender's Number. | Day of Month. | In reply to Number. | A A A |
| Q1/2 | 1.7.17 | | |

Herewith attached War Diary for Month of June 1917.

From 14th Machine Gun Company
Place
Time

The above may be forwarded as now corrected. (Z)

Censor. Signature of Addressee or person authorised to telegraph in his name. Lieut

WAR DIARY of No 2 Machine Gun Company.

INTELLIGENCE SUMMARY.

Army Form C. 2118.

Ref Sheet 66E & 66D 20 & 10
Nightingale 5A 10-6 5-2-a

Place	Date	Hour	Summary of Events and Information	Remarks and references to Appendices
MARCELCAVE	June 1st		Company paraded at 12.30 AM to entrain. Transport here successfully entrained at 1 AM by which time the Company arrived at Station. Train started at 2:30 AM and arrived at its destination BAILLEUL at 3 PM. After a successful detrainment the Company arrived in billets at A.21.a.6.8.(1 mile west of STEENWERCK) at 5.10 PM.	BSN
A21a.6.8.	2.6.17		At 2:15 PM, the four sections with guns proceeded to take over Anti-aircraft defences on the various dumps E of BAILLEUL. All guns were in position by 4 P.M.	BSN
A21a.6.8.	3.6.17		31 guns M.G. Coy relieved 114th Coy on Anti-aircraft defences on the various dumps E of BAILLEUL. Relief complete by 4 PM. All teams arriving in billets at A.21.a.6.8.(about) by 6 PM.	BSN
A21.a.6.8	4.6.17		Company in billets training. The Commanding Officer and Section Officers made a reconnaissance of the enemy line at MESSINES.	BSN

S. Stanfuin
1st Lieut M.G.C

WAR DIARY of 5th R Machine Gun Company

INTELLIGENCE SUMMARY

Army Form C. 2118

(Erase heading not required.)

Place	Date	Hour	Summary of Events and Information	Remarks and references to Appendices
A21.6.8	5.6.17		Company in billets training.	Ref. Sheet Sheet 57A 1/40000
A21.6.8	6.6.17		Company in billets training.	
A21.6.8	7.6.17		Company in billets training. 2/Lieut A.H.Link joined Company from Machine Gun Base Depot.	
A21.6.8	8.6.17		Company in billets training. Lieut N. Ferguson joined Company from 111th Machine Gun Company. Appointed S.O.	
A21.6.8	9.6.17		Company in billets training.	
A21.6.9	10.6.17		Company in billet training. Capt E. Ridley proceeded to Genn. Harr. Course for duty.	
A21.6.8	11.6.17		Company in billets training. "A" Section attended presentation of T.C.Ribbon by Brig Gen Y.N. Lunsden C.B.S.O 60th & 111th Infantry Brigade	

W. Mr. Burt
Capt
5th R. MG Co

Army Form C. 2118.

WAR DIARY of 111th Machine Gun Coy.
or
INTELLIGENCE SUMMARY.
(Erase heading not required.)

Instructions regarding War Diaries and Intelligence Summaries are contained in F.S. Regs., Part II. and the Staff Manual respectively. Title pages will be prepared in manuscript.

Place	Date	Hour	Summary of Events and Information	Remarks and references to Appendices
A 21.b	12.6.17		Company in billets preparing for march	Sheet Hazebrouck 5A France 36.5.27.19 north BBA
A 27.b.8.12.6.17 Vieux-Berquin	13.6.17		At 11.45AM Company moved to the EECKE AREA. Route via VIEUX-BERQUIN - STRAZEELE - CAESTRES and arrived at 11.5 P.M.	BBA
EECKE	14.6.17		Company in billets training. At 10 AM Transport moved under firm S.S. North to HIRONDOUDT? area	BBA
EECKE TETEGHEM	15.6.17		Company enbussed at 4.45 AM en route for TETEGHEM, arriving at 10.10 AM. Transport arriving at 6.10 PM	BBA
TETEGHEM	16.6.17		Company in billets. Sea bathing in afternoon	BBA

5.5 Luck Kus
Lt M.G.C.

Army Form C. 2118.

WAR DIARY of 10th Machine Gun Coy
or
INTELLIGENCE SUMMARY
(Erase heading not required.)

Instructions regarding War Diaries and Intelligence Summaries are contained in F. S. Regs., Part II. and the Staff Manual respectively. Title pages will be prepared in manuscript.

Place	Date	Hour	Summary of Events and Information	Remarks and references to Appendices
TETEGHEM			Ref Sheet 1a 1:5,000. Sheet 12 S.M. 1:40,000.	
COXYDE	31.7.17		Company embarqued at DUNKERQUE at 8 a.m. and proceeded via Canal thro' to FURNES. Train there by march route to Camp No 49 arriving at 5.30 P.M. Transport moved across Fields & R' arriving at COXYDE via MALHOUCK-ADINKIRKE and LA PANNE arr. 5.30 P.M. Train Spent at 1.15 PM. Company went for Bathing.	65M 65M
COXYDE	1.8.17		Company in billets. Passed for Sea Bathing at 10 P.M.	65M
COXYDE	19.8.17		Advance Liaison M.G. Section in "C" Sub Sector NIEUPORT at night. Relief being complete by 2am 20th. Distribution as follows:- Company HQ at NIEUPORT. Transport at CAMP 49 COXYDE. A.B.C and E Sections in the line (7th Sub Sector)	65M 65M
NIEUPORT	24.8.17		Sections in the line. Casualties Nil. Weather changeable	

WAR DIARY of 14th Machine Gun Company

INTELLIGENCE SUMMARY

Army Form C. 2118.

Instructions regarding War Diaries and Intelligence Summaries are contained in F.S. Regs., Part II. and the Staff Manual respectively. Title pages will be prepared in manuscript.

(Erase heading not required.)

Ref Sheet 1/2,500 & 20,000

Place	Date	Hour	Summary of Events and Information	Remarks and references to Appendices
NIEUPORT	24/6/17		6 x ORs permanently attached Company in the line. Casualties Nil. Nieuport fine day. Company Headquarters established at NIEUPORT.	A.S.H.
NIEUPORT	25/6/17		Company in the line. Casualties Nil. Nieuport fine.	A.S.H.
NIEUPORT	26/6/17		Company in the line. Casualties Nil. Weather fine.	A.S.H.
NIEUPORT	24/6/17		Company in the line. Casualties Nil. Weather fine.	A.S.H.
NIEUPORT	25/6/17		Company in the line. Casualties Nil. Weather fine.	A.S.H.
NIEUPORT	26/6/17		Company relieved on the night of 26/27th by 99th M.G. Coy in "C" Sub Sector. Relief completed by 11.30 pm. On relief sections marched to Teph BART CAMP COXYDE.	A.S.H.

E.D. Cook Capt
14 Coy M.G.C.

Army Form C. 2118.

WAR DIARY of 1/1 Motor Machine Gun Bty

or

INTELLIGENCE SUMMARY.

(Erase heading not required.)

Instructions regarding War Diaries and Intelligence Summaries are contained in F. S. Regs., Part II. and the Staff Manual respectively. Title pages will be prepared in manuscript.

Place	Date	Hour	Summary of Events and Information	Remarks and references to Appendices
COXYDE	27/6/17		Company in billets resting. Sea bathing in afternoon.	
COXYDE	28/6/17		Company in billets training. Sea bathing in afternoon. Enq Trench actg.	
NIEUPORT	29/6/17		At 6 PM Company less Transport moved up to NIEUPORT and Sections proceeded to the line where they relieved 219th M.G.Coy in "A" and "B" Sub Sectors. Relief completed at 11 PM. Coy Headquarters established at NIEUPORT.	
NIEUPORT	30/6/17		Distribution of Company as follows:- A B C and D Sections in the line. (As G. Sub Sector) Trench Mt. Casualties Nil.	

E.A. West [signature]
OC Motor [signature]

Army Form C. 2118.

WAR DIARY of 114th Machine Gun Coy

INTELLIGENCE SUMMARY.

(Erase heading not required.)

Vol 18

Place	Date	Hour	Summary of Events and Information	Remarks and references to Appendices
			BELGIUM By Sheet 12 SW & Sheet 19 1/40,000	
NIEUPORT	1st/4/19		Company in the line. Distribution as follows. A, B, C, and D Sections in D and E Sub Sectors. Weather was wet. Casualties nil.	M Lt
NIEUPORT	2/4/19		Company in line. Weather fine. Casualties Nil	MB Lt
NIEUPORT	3/4/19		Company in line. Weather fine. 4 O.Rs Wounded	MB Lt
NIEUPORT	4/4/19		Company in line. Weather fine. 1 O.R. Wounded.	MB Lt
NIEUPORT	5/4/19		Company in line. Weather fine. 1 O.R. Wounded.	MB Lt
NIEUPORT & COXYDE	6/4/19		Company was relieved by 96th M.G. Coy in D and E Sub-Sectors. On relief Company marched by sections independently to JEAN BART Camp at COXYDE. Relief was completed by 11.15 p.m. Weather fine.	MB Lt

WAR DIARY of 4 with Machine Gun Company

INTELLIGENCE SUMMARY

Army Form C. 2118.

Place	Date	Hour	Summary of Events and Information	Remarks and references to Appendices
COXYDE	7.4.19		BELGIUM SHEET 12 S.W. & SHEET 11 S.E. Company in billets. Weather fine. Casualties Nil.	JB
COXYDE	8.4.19		Company in billets training. Weather fine. Casualties Nil. Company Pay Parade.	JB
COXYDE	9.4.19		Company in billets training. Weather fine. Casualties Nil.	JB
COXYDE & X6a.3.8. SHEET 11A.SE 1/20,000	10.4.19		B&C Sections proceeded as a working party to X6.A.3.8. Remainder of Cy in billets training. At 9.30 p.m. Company was marked up in reserve. Usual Company details remained behind in JEAN BART CAMP. 1.O.R. Murrell. 1 Light Draught (No 3) killed by Shrapnel. 1 Light Draught (No 69) Murrell.	JB
X6a3.8. SHEET 11A.SE 1/20,000	11.4.19		Company still held in reserve at CAMP RABAILLET. Weather fair. Casualties Nil.	JB
X6a.3.8.	12.4.19		Company still held in reserve at Camp RABAILLET. Weather fair. Casualties Nil.	JB

2353 Wt. W3544/1454 700,000 5/15 D.D. & L. A.D.S.S.Forms/C. 2118.

WAR DIARY
INTELLIGENCE SUMMARY.

Army Form C. 2118.

4 th Marine Gun Company

(Erase heading not required.)

Instructions regarding War Diaries and Intelligence Summaries are contained in F. S. Regs., Part II. and the Staff Manual respectively. Title pages will be prepared in manuscript.

Place	Date	Hour	Summary of Events and Information	Remarks and references to Appendices
X.6.a.3.8. & NIEUPORT	13.4.17		Offset 12.5M Zero. Company move up to NIEUPORT at 9pm to relieve 94th M.G. Coy. Enemy bombarded very heavily with Gas Shells. Coy to Ors established at NIEUPORT 2.30 am 14.4.17. Casualties 1 Officer killed 1 Officer wounded. 15 ORs wounded. 3 ORs joined from Base Depot.	A
NIEUPORT	14.4.17		Company in lines C Sector Casualties NIL. WEATHER FAIR.	B N
NIEUPORT	15.4.17		Company in line. Casualties NIL Weather good.	B 16
NIEUPORT	16.4.17		Company in line. Casualties NIL Weather good.	B 17
NIEUPORT	17.4.17		Company in line. Casualties NIL Weather very good.	B 18
NIEUPORT	18.4.17		Company in line. 5 ORs joined from Base Depot. Casualties NIL. Weather very good.	B 19

Army Form C. 2118.

WAR DIARY of 14th Machine Gun Company
INTELLIGENCE SUMMARY.

(Erase heading not required.)

Instructions regarding War Diaries and Intelligence Summaries are contained in F.S. Regs., Part II. and the Staff Manual respectively. Title pages will be prepared in manuscript.

Place	Date	Hour	Summary of Events and Information	Remarks and references to Appendices
			Belgium & France Sheet 12 Sh. Sheet 11 20. 8.10 BELGIUM & FRANCE SHEET 19	
NIEUPORT	19/4/17		Company in line. At 9pm Coy was relieved by 148th M.G. Coy in C & E Sectors. Sections on relief marched independently to Jean Bart Camp. Relief was completed by 12.30am 19/20.4.17. 2 O.R. Wounded.	C.B. JB
COXYDE B.			Company marched to LEFFRINGHOUCKE at billets at No 11 Farm. 2 Officers joined from M.G. Base. 13 O.R. reinforcements from Base Depot. Casualties Nil. Weather warm.	C.B. JB
LEFFRINGHOUCKE 20.4.17 C.29.C.1.1.				
LEFFRINGHOUCKE 21/4/17 C.29. C.1.1			Company in billets resting. Day was spent in cleaning up. Casualties Nil. Weather good.	C.B. JB
LEFFRINGHOUCKE 22.4.17 C.29. C.1.1.			Company in billets. Coy attend devotions under the various denominations. Weather very good. 3 O.R. joined from Base Depot. Casualties Nil.	C.B. JB
LEFFRINGHOUCKE 23.4.17 C.20.C.1.1			Company paraded at 8am and proceeded to Sea Beach at C1.30.a.25 for practice inspection. Coy returned to billets at 1pm. Casualties Nil. Weather good.	C.B. JB

2353 Wt. W2544/1454 700,000 5/15 D.D. & L. A.D.S.S./Forms/C. 2118.

Army Form C. 2118.

WAR DIARY
or
INTELLIGENCE SUMMARY.

(Erase heading not required.)

11th Machine Gun Company
Belgium and France
H.Q. and

Instructions regarding War Diaries and Intelligence Summaries are contained in F. S. Regs., Part II. and the Staff Manual respectively. Title pages will be prepared in manuscript.

Place	Date	Hour	Summary of Events and Information	Remarks and references to Appendices
LEFFRINGHOUCK C29.c.11.	24/4/17		Company paraded at 9am and marched to See Bruges at C.13.a.25. At 9.45 am Brigade was inspected by Maj/Gen Shute G.O.C. 32nd Division. At 10.20 am Brigade was inspected by the XV Corps Commander. 7 O.R.s joined from Base Dépôt. Weather Good. Casualties Nil.	CB
LEFFRINGHOUCK C.29.C.11.	25/4/17		Company in Billets training. Weather fair. Casualties Nil.	CB
LEFFRINGHOUCK C.29.C.11.	26/4/17		Company in Billets training. Weather good. Casualties. 1 O.R. Accidentally wounded.	CB
LEFFRINGHOUCK C.29.C.11.	27/4/17		Company in Billets training. Weather fair. Casualties Nil	CB
LEFFRINGHOUCK C.29.C.11.	28/4/17		Company in Billets training. Weather good. Casualties Nil	CB
LEFFRINGHOUCK C.29.C.11.	29/4/17		Company in Billets training. Weather fair. Casualties Nil	CB
LEFFRINGHOUCK C.29.o.11	30/4/17		Company in Billets training. Weather fair. Casualties Nil	CB
LEFFRINGHOUCK C.29.o.11	3/4/17		Company in Billets training. Weather fair. Casualties Nil	CB
LEFFRINGHOUCK C.29.o.11	2/4/17		Company moved to C.21.a for Brigade practice "Known" attack	CB
LEFFRINGHOUCK C.29.o.11	3/4/17			

Army Form C. 2118.

WAR DIARY
or
INTELLIGENCE SUMMARY.

(Erase heading not required.)

11th Machine Gun Company

Reference Sheets N.S.E. 1/40000 1/2 3 etc. 1/10.000

Place	Date	Hour	Summary of Events and Information	Remarks and references to Appendices
LEFERINGHOUCKE	1.8.17		Company in billets preparing for move. Casualties Nil. Weather very wet.	
C.29.d.1.1.	2.8.17		Company moved with 114th Infantry Bde group to COXYDE area arriving at CAMP No. 90 at 6.30 p.m. Weather very wet.	
COXYDE	3.8.17		Company moved from CAMP No. 90 at 3.25 p.m. and marched to billets COXYDE arriving at 4.50 p.m. Weather very wet. Lieut S.S. WORTH rejoined company from leave U.K.	
COXYDE	4.8.17		Company in billets. Evening Weather fine. Casualties Nil.	
COXYDE	5.8.17		A.B.C & D Sections employed on the line making indirect fire positions and establishing ammunition dumps preparatory to forthcoming operations. Weather fine. Casualties 1 O.R. wounded by shell fire at M.35.C.2.4.	65 OR wounded

Army Form C. 2118.

WAR DIARY
or
INTELLIGENCE SUMMARY. 11th Machine Gun Company

(Erase heading not required.)

Place	Date	Hour	Summary of Events and Information	Remarks and references to Appendices
			Ref Sheets BELGIUM 18 1/20,000 & OOST DUNKERKE II 1/20,000	
COXYDE.	6.8.17		Two teams of "C" Section under Lt A.H.D. FAIRBARNS established B Anti-aircraft positions at the following points :– 1 Gun at M32.A.5.4. and 1 Gun at S2.B.3.9. Weather fine. Casualties Nil. 2 O.R.a reinforcements arrived from M.G. Base Depot CAMIERS.	
COXYDE	7.8.17		Two teams of "A" Section on Anti-aircraft positions Remained ∧ Company in WULIPE COXYDE. Weather fine. Casualties Nil.	
COXYDE.	8.8.17		Distribution of Company as on the 7th inst. Casualties Nil. Weather fine.	
COXYDE.	9.8.17		Distribution of Company as on the 8th inst. Casualties Nil. Weather fine.	

Army Form C. 2118.

WAR DIARY
INTELLIGENCE SUMMARY 147th Machine Gun Company

(Erase heading not required.)

Place	Date	Hour	Summary of Events and Information	Remarks and references to Appendices
COXYDE.	10.8.17		Ref Sheets BELGIUM 12 S.E. 1/20.000 WEST DUNKERKE 11. 1/20.000 Distribution of Company as on the 9th inst. Weather fine. Casualties Nil.	
COXYDE.	11.8.17		2 Sections of Company relieved 2 Sections of the 219th M.G. Company. Relief was completed by 11 p.m. Forward Company H. Qrs. were established at NIEUPORT N/28 C 80.2.4. Remainder of Company remained in billets at COXYDE. Weather fine. Casualties Nil.	
Rear H. Qrs. COXYDE. Forward H. Qrs. NIEUPORT N.28 C. 80.2.4	12.8.17		2 Sections in the line. Remainder of Company in billets COXYDE. Weather fine. Casualties Nil. 1.O.R. proceeded to M.G.C. I.O. to attend 5th Instructional Staff Course. E.B. North	

WAR DIARY
INTELLIGENCE SUMMARY. 14th N. Machine Gun Corps

Army Form C. 2118.

(Erase heading not required.)

Place	Date	Hour	Summary of Events and Information	Remarks and references to Appendices
Regt H.Q. Coxyde	13.8.17		Ref Sheets Belgium 1:20,000 OOST DUNKERKE 11 1/20,000 Distribution of Company as on the 12th inst.	
Forward H.Q. Nieuport			Casualties Lieut G.B.M. REED wounded by shell fire 1 O.R killed 1 O.R wounded	
M.28.c.20.2.7				
D°	14.8.17		Distribution of Company as on the 13th inst. Casualties 4 O.R.s Killed 2 H.O.R.s wounded by shell landing in Cellule COXYDE (X.13.B.2.8)	
D°	15.8.17		Distribution of Company as on the 14th inst. Nothing to report. Casualties Nil.	
D°	16.8.17		D°	
Q.22.B.2.8	16.8.17		A & B Sections Rear H.Qrs and transport at 11.15 am moved from COXYDE to Camp at Q.22.B.2.8 arriving at 11.50 A.m	

Army Form C. 2118.

WAR DIARY
or
INTELLIGENCE SUMMARY. 14th Machine Gun Company
(Erase heading not required.)

Instructions regarding War Diaries and Intelligence Summaries are contained in F. S. Regs., Part II. and the Staff Manual respectively. Title pages will be prepared in manuscript.

Place	Date	Hour	Summary of Events and Information	Remarks and references to Appendices
Regt. H.Q. W.22.B.2.8.	14.8.17		Ref. Sheets BELGIUM 12.S.W./20.000 OOST DUINKERKE II./20.000 11.S.E. 1/10.000 & 1/20.000	
Forward H.Q. NIEUPORT N.28 C.80.24.			Two sections in the line were relieved by two sections of the 243rd Machine Gun Company. Relief was completed by 11.30 p.m. On relief sections withdrew to Webbs at W.17 c.5.4. Casualties Nil.	
Camp at W.22.B.2.8.	15.8.17		Whole Company in Webbs resting. Weather fine.	
Camp at W.22.B.2.8.	18.8.17		Working party of 70 O.R's under Lieuts G.R. DAVIDSON and W.C. BROWN were supplied to 14th Infantry Brigade.	
Camp at W.22.B.2.8.	19.8.17		Divine services were attended by the different denominations of the Company.	

Army Form C. 2118.

WAR DIARY
or
INTELLIGENCE SUMMARY. 114th Machine Gun Company

(Erase heading not required.)

Place	Date	Hour	Summary of Events and Information	Remarks and references to Appendices
Camp at W.22.c.2.8.	20.8.17		Ref Sheet 11.S.E. 1/20.000	
			Company in Lewis Gun Training	
		8.A.M. to 8.45A.M. Physical training.	
		9 a.m. to 12.30 p.m. Barrage Drill on Beach LA PANNE.	
		2 p.m. to 6.3 p.m. Gas Drill.	
		6 p.m. Short lecture.	
Camp at W.22.c.2.8.	21.8.17		Company in Lewis Gun Training	
		8.A.M. to 8.45A.M. Close Order Drill.	
		9.A.M. to 12.30 P.M. Firing short range (W22.d.5.4.)	
Camp at W.22.c.2.8.	22.8.17		Company in Lewis Gun Training	
		8.A.M. to 8.45A.M. Rifle exercises & saluting.	
		9 A.M. to 12.30 P.M. Practice laying for direction.	
		Maps & compass work. Instruction on the use of auxiliary.	
		Aiming screen.	

WAR DIARY
of
INTELLIGENCE SUMMARY. 14th Machine Gun Company.

Army Form C. 2118.

(Erase heading not required.)

Place	Date	Hour	Summary of Events and Information	Remarks and references to Appendices
Camp at W.22.B.2.8.	23.8.17		Ref Sheet 11 SE 1/20.000	
			Company in billets training.	
		8.30 a.m. to 12.30 p.m.	Barrage practice on Beach LA PANNE	
		2.0 p.m. to 5.0 p.m.	Cleaning guns, harness etc	
		6.0 p.m.	Lecture	
Camp at W.22.B.2.8.	24.8.17		Company in billets training.	
		8.0 a.m. to 12.30 p.m.	Barrage practice on Beach LA PANNE.	
		9.30 p.m. to 11.0 p.m.	Night Operations	
Camp at W.22.B.25.N	25.8.17		Company in billets training	
		8.0 a.m. to 8.45 a.m.	Physical Drill.	
		9.0 a.m. to 11.0 a.m.	1st Coy Barrage Drill	
		" " " "	Firing on Range	
		11.0 a.m. to 1.0 p.m.	Barrage Drill	
		" " " "	Firing on Range	

WAR DIARY
INTELLIGENCE SUMMARY. 14th Machine Gun Company

Army Form C. 2118.

(Erase heading not required.)

Ref Sheet 11. S.E. 1/20,000

Place	Date	Hour	Summary of Events and Information	Remarks and references to Appendices
Camp at W.22.B.2.8.	26.8.17		Company attended Divine Services.	
		6 & 16 C of E 10.15 a.m		
		Presbyterians 10.0 a.m		
		R.C. 8.45 a.m.		
Camp at W.22.B.2.8.	27/8/17		Operation Orders were received at 3 a.m. for 32nd Division to relieve the 33rd Division in the line.	
AUSTRALIA CAMP R.Q.R.			Company paraded at 8.30 a.m. and marched to little AUSTRALIA CAMP arriving there at 10.5 a.m.	
H.Q.		5.30 p.m	A & B Sections reconnoitred Nieuport and moved into the line and Nieuport respectively and relieved 2 Sections of 19th M.G. Company, this relief was quiet and effected by 10.0 p.m. Casualties Nil.	
NIEUPORT Forward H.Q. (M/34.a.8.5.)			Weather very wet.	
	27.8.17		Lieut. G.B. DALLAS & 20 R'os paraded in charge of ammunition in Aircraft defence at 14th Corps R.F.C. Works.	

Army Form C. 2118.

WAR DIARY
or
INTELLIGENCE SUMMARY. 164th Machine Gun Coy
(Erase heading not required.)

Instructions regarding War Diaries and Intelligence Summaries are contained in F. S. Regs., Part II. and the Staff Manual respectively. Title pages will be prepared in manuscript.

Place	Date	Hour	Summary of Events and Information	Remarks and references to Appendices
AUSTRALIA CAMP (REAR H.Q.)	27.8.17		Ref/Maps BELGIUM S.W. 1/20,000 OOST DUNKERKE N.S.E. 1/20,000 B.C. Sections at AUSTRALIA CAMP handed at 6.15 a.m. marched to the line and relieved there 2 Sections of the 248th M.G. Company. This relief was completed by 11 p.m. without casualties. Weather very stormy. 2nd Lieut. G.B. DALLAS recalled from Anti-aircraft course.	
NIEUPORT M.34.a.8.5. (FORWARD H.Q.) To	28.8.17		A.B.C & D. Sections in the line, forward H. Qrs NIEUPORT. Details, Rear H. Qrs and Transport at AUSTRALIA CAMP COXYDE. During the whole day the COXYDE AREA was intermittently shelled. At 3.25 p.m. a shell landed in company transport lines causing casualties as follows:- 1. O.R. wounded and died of wounds. 5. O.Rs. wounded. 1. light draught horse killed, 1. L.D. wounded and 2 killed. Weather very stormy.	

Army Form C. 2118.

WAR DIARY
INTELLIGENCE SUMMARY — 14th A.I. Machine Gun Company
(Erase heading not required.)

Place	Date	Hour	Summary of Events and Information	Remarks and references to Appendices
AUSTRALIA	30.8.17		Ref Sheets Belgium S.W. 1/20,000 OOST DUNKERKE 11 S.E. 1/20,000	
CAMP COYDE			Distribution of Company as on the 29th inst.	
(REAR H.Q.)			Nothing to report. Casualties Nil. Weather showery	
NIEUPORT				
M SH "8.5				
(FORWARD H.Q.)				
Do	31.8.17		Distribution of Company as on the 30th inst. The undermentioned officers of the Company attended lecture on new Machine Gun Barrage at IX Corps Schools. Lt. S.S. WORTH. " D.C. BROWN. 2/Lt. E.H. DALLAS. " H. ROTHWELL. Casualties Nil. Weather fine.	

CONFIDENTIAL

WAR DIARY of 4th Company Machine Gun Corps

INTELLIGENCE SUMMARY. By Lieut. H.E. Belgium.

Army Form C. 2118.

20,000

G2061 1 OCT 1917 4th INFANTRY BRIGADE

Place	Date	Hour	Summary of Events and Information	Remarks and references to Appendices
COY H.QRT.S. NIEUPORT	1st Sept 1917		Company in the line. Transport and details now arrived back at COXYDE	B. M. Hunt
TRANSPORT AT AUSTRALIA CAMP				
COY HQRT at NIEUPORT	2 Sept 1917		Casualties L/Cpl Wounded. Neuton Jun	B. M. Hunt
TRANSPORT AT AUSTRALIA CAMP			Company in the line. Transport and details at COXYDE. Casualties nil. Neuton niff 92th	B. M. Hunt
COXYDE COY H.QRT.S. NIEUPORT	3rd Sept 1917		Distribution of Company as on the 2nd inst. Nil casualties. Neuton nil.	B. M. Hunt
TRANSPORT AT AUSTRALIA CAMP				
COXYDE COY H.QRT at NIEUPORT	4 Sept 1917		Company in the line. Transport and details at COXYDE. 4 O.R.s been wounded while carrying rations in NIEUPORT. Neuton fire	B. M. Hunt
TRANSPORT AT AUSTRALIA CAMP				
COXYDE				
COY H.QRT.S. NIEUPORT	5 Sept 1917		Distribution of Company as on the 4th inst. Re about 10 PM. a hostile air raid was made on AUSTRALIA and CANADA CAMPS. 3 Bombs were dropped in AUSTRALIA CAMP and six in CANADA CAMP. 25 casualties were inflicted on the 219th M.G.C. and 13 Lancashire Fusiliers. No neutral no casualties.	B. M. Hunt
REAR H.QRT at AUSTRALIA CAMP				
COXYDE				

CONFIDENTIAL

WAR DIARY or INTELLIGENCE SUMMARY.
(Erase heading not required.)

Army Form C. 2118.

of 2nd Coy Machine Gun Corps.

Ref: Sheet 56 II Belgium 20,000

Place	Date	Hour	Summary of Events and Information	Remarks and references to Appendices
Coy H. Qrs. NIEUPORT	12/Sept 17		Company in the line (Lombartzyde sector) No casualties	
Band HQ AUSTRALIA CAMP COXYDE			Hutted very good.	
Coy H. Qrs. NIEUPORT	Sept 14		Company in the line. At about 11.25 P.M. the enemy shelled POST RANIA CAMP	
Rem: of Coy at AUSTRALIA CAMP COXYDE			One still sites of shelling from Austria Hill. Casualties amongst [?]	
			Company were increasing casualties as follows 1/R Killed 1/25 wounded	
			2 Lt Pl Gnaughtness killed, 1 Lt Gnaughtness slightly wounded	
			1/R wounded in the leg	
Coy Hqrs at NIEUPORT			Distribution of company as on 9 inst. Weather was very good.	
Details at AUSTRALIA CAMP COXYDE	Sept 15/17		No casualties.	
Coy H Qrs NIEUPORT	Sept 16/17		Distribution of company as on 8 inst. Casualties nil. Bruce Martin a gunner that Lost [?] of the 117 1 Manchester Regt. returned to this unit	
NIEUPORT	Sept 17/17		Company in the line. No casualties. Weather good.	
NIEUPORT	Sept 18/17		Company in the line. Casualties nil. Weather good.	

CONFIDENTIAL

WAR DIARY
or
INTELLIGENCE SUMMARY

Army Form C. 2118.

7th Coy Machine Gun Corps
Ref Sheet 15W Belgium 20.S.W.

(Erase heading not required.)

Place	Date	Hour	Summary of Events and Information	Remarks and references to Appendices
Bef Agnes at NIEUPORT	Sept 12.17		Company in line (LOMBARTZYDE SECTOR). Casualties L/Cpl E.D.C. Stewart wounded in action. 1 O.R. Wounded in action. Weather fine.	
Coy H.Qrs. NIEUPORT REAR H.Qrs. AUSTRALIA CAMP	Sept 13th		Company were relieved by 96th M.G.C. in LOMBARTZYDE SECTOR on the night of 13/14th. The relief was successfully completed without any casualties by 9.30 P.M. Company diaries marches back independently to AUSTRALIA CAMP. The last section arrived in Camp at about midnight.	
AUSTRALIA CAMP COXYDE.	Sept 14th 15th 16th		Company in billets cleaning guns, equipment etc. 2 teams of "D" Section under 2/Lt E.H. Dallas relieves 2 Teams of 219th M.G. Coy of Anti-aircraft positions at M.32.A.7.t. and M.32.B.4.9. Relief was completed by 6 P.M.
The Company relieved the 96th M.G. Coy in the following Anti-aircraft positions.
X.13.C. 50.25 }
X.13.C.H.0. 50. } to protect railway and dump near HET-LEI-HAE FARM and Camp
X.13.A. 35.15 }
X.13.A. 10.10. } to protect Camps in DUNES, AUSTRALIA & CANADA CAMP, and CROSS Roads.
W.13.C.
These guns were mounted at dawn (Samland dismounted at dusk (P.M.)	

CONFIDENTIAL

Army Form C. 2118.

WAR DIARY
or
INTELLIGENCE SUMMARY.

(Erase heading not required.)

Instructions regarding War Diaries and Intelligence Summaries are contained in F. S. Regs., Part II. and the Staff Manual respectively. Title pages will be prepared in manuscript.

Place	Date	Hour	Summary of Events and Information	Remarks and references to Appendices
AUSTRALIA CAMP OUVRDE	Sept 1917			
AUSTRALIA CAMP OXYDE	Sept 1917			
AUSTRALIA CAMP OXYDE	Sept 1917			
AUSTRALIA CAMP OXYDE	Sept 1917			

CONFIDENTIAL

WAR DIARY

or

INTELLIGENCE SUMMARY.

(Erase heading not required.)

Army Form C. 2118.

4th Aust. 5th M.G. Battalion.

Place	Date	Hour	Summary of Events and Information	Remarks and references to Appendices
Australian Camp Oxford	Feb 1/18		Capt. Harrison left S.S. North for Country for 3rd Division	By boat
			Rds struck a German station with "K.J." Everything ok	
			Aniston "Hans" bright at 7 pm at N.W. 22.6 O.P.S from #F.S.D	
			Drivers hired infantry hire #H.T.D	
Australian Camp Oxford	Feb 10/18		Company at Billets Having Breakfast 5:30 am 6:3 & 6:15am Strenuous	Bombing
		12.46.5 pm Orders being handed in winter Nubana Company	
			Orders in N.S. 2nd Div. heavy Name Iquara	
			Human Company instructions received & divisional orders	
			to be sent to La Panne Capt Harrison to S.S. North	
			Attend a Conference Returns immediately office arm	
			New 10th (2nd Div) one set to left of hills to 33rd SDE	
			1st Bgde (4th C.R.)	
Australian Camp Oxford	Feb 20/18		Company on British Breaking in more will be here	Bombing
			2 lent with new Lieut A.S. Sides Harrison returns	
			M.36.5 65.8 M.29.6 O.P.10 set at return of 2 Lens I.214	

CONFIDENTIAL

Army Form C. 2118.

WAR DIARY
or
INTELLIGENCE SUMMARY.

(Erase heading not required.)

Lightly Machine Gun Corp
Antwerpen & Merry
BEF RUSSELL Billionaire 20

Place	Date	Hour	Summary of Events and Information	Remarks and references to Appendices
HOSTRUM CAMP COXYDE	Sept 3rd 1917		200th Machine Gun Company	
COXYDE CAMP	Sept 21st	2.30pm	Nr. 2, 3 & 4 Companies marched out B.M. Stop new road to Three Kings	
COXYDE TERRE			No. 3 A 3.55.50 arriving at abt 4.15 pm. 1st & 3rd m Company headquarters
moved via COXYDE – OOST-DUNKIRK – ZOUAVE ROAD to THREE KINGS	
KINGS FARM M.32.D.3.1.		7pm	Out with Nr 3i Shot 4 O.R. were at 6.30 pm. No 53 am F.B.C. Out D Sections with highline limbers made haze t Section Limber
Officers marched via COXYDE – OOST-DUNKIRK – Road to LES FITZ 1600 Section's lost route, returned to P.W.R. Machine gun limbers the relief to
positions by 1.50 pm without any casualties. Reliefs were re-adjusted and made as follows at 9pm N.G Coy at COXYDE was relieved by L.B Coy and and
landed out to 9yr N.G Coy in L.Myers farm at LB Coy and 7pm at L.B. 3.10.4.5. 146 & 6.15 respectively	Lamboard
THREE KINGS FARM M.32.D.31.	Sept 22nd		Company in the line as scattered. No weather poor.
A&C Griffin and L R pieces company from Michigan on sand	

Army Form C. 2118.

WAR DIARY
INTELLIGENCE SUMMARY
(Erase heading not required.)

Place	Date	Hour	Summary of Events and Information	Remarks and references to Appendices
THREE KINGS FARM	Sbr 23rd		[illegible handwritten entries]	
M.32.D.3.b.			Section turned over M.36.D (BOMBART TYPE 20,0,0) [illegible]... the whole of [illegible]...	
			[illegible]...	Signed [illegible]
THREE KINGS FARM	Sbr 26th		Another machine [illegible]...	Signed [illegible]
M.32.D.3.b.			Company in the line [illegible]...	
THREE KINGS FARM	Sbr 27th		Company in the line [illegible]...	Signed [illegible]
M.32.D.3.b.				

CONFIDENTIAL.

Army Form C. 2118.

WAR DIARY
or
INTELLIGENCE SUMMARY.

(Erase heading not required.)

Instructions regarding War Diaries and Intelligence Summaries are contained in F. S. Regs., Part II. and the Staff Manual respectively. Title pages will be prepared in manuscript.

War Diary of 11th Coy Machine Gun Corps

Place	Date	Hour	Summary of Events and Information	Remarks and references to Appendices
TURCO FARM				
FARM N.32.D.3.1	Sept 20th		Company in line. Situation nil. Weather very wet. At 11 am our artillery placed a barrage on the German line. 12 n our own artillery received a hostile SOS call. The line had not been cut. No casualties on our side were incurred.	[initials]
THREE KINGS FARM M.3a.D2.1.	Sept 21st		Company in line. The enemy commenced a very heavy artillery bombardment at 6.30am his his line. Our infantry lines the SOS signal which was promptly taken up by our artillery. Our fire was extremely severe and the enemy was almost at once has movement to stop but our artillery maintained a heavy barrage. During the lighter front up through the stage of the situation was again normal. Casualties NIL Nunnon	[initials]

Army Form C. 2118.

WAR DIARY
or
INTELLIGENCE SUMMARY.

(Erase heading not required.)

WAR DIARY Gunkley Machine Gun Company
of 6th Sect Machine Gun Co.

Place	Date	Hour	Summary of Events and Information	Remarks and references to Appendices
M.16.b.65.35			1 Company in line.	B. May 20
M.21.b.	May 29th		Machines that attacked by our aircraft and came low down in places over the enemy's line	
M.14.b.65.55	May 30th		Nos. known to fire. Casualties nil.	B. May 30
M.20.d.61.97	May 31st		Machines moves up into front of our positions at M.29.c.30.60.	B. May 31
M.20.d.31.	"		Arrangements have established in new positions by 9.45 pm	
M.21.c.30.60	"		No cars situation whole as usual during the night	
M.20.d.61.97 M.20.d.31. M.21.c.30.60	June 1st		Enemy in front in line. Casualties nil. Nothing gained.	June 1

S.S. North Lieut.
6th Div Machine Gun Corps.

Confidential

WAR DIARY of Employ Machine Gun Corps
INTELLIGENCE SUMMARY

(Erase heading not required.) of 2nd Bar. Belgium N.52. 20,000

Army Form C. 2118.

WO/21

Place	Date	Hour	Summary of Events and Information	Remarks and references to Appendices
HD QRS AT M.29.C.20.60	Oct 1st 1917		Company in line in ST GEORGES SECTOR. Weather good. Casualties nil	WA
HD QRS AT M.29.C.20.60	Oct 2nd 1917		Company in line. Weather good. Casualties nil	WA
HD QRS AT M.29.C.20.60	Oct 3rd 1917		Company in line. Weather inclement. Casualties nil	WA
HD QRS AT M.29.C.20.60	Oct 4th 1917		Company on the line. Weather wet and a trifle cold. Casualties nil	WA
HD QRS AT M.29.C.20.60	Oct 5th 1917		Company in the line. Weather fine. Casualties nil	WA
HD QRS AT M.29.C.20.60	Oct 6th 1917		Company in the line. Weather wet. Battalions of the Brigade were relieved by 176th Infantry Brigade in ST GEORGES SECTOR. Casualties 1 OR wounded.	WA
HD QRS AT M.29.C.20.60	Oct 7th 1917		Company in line. Weather very wet. Company was relieved by 176th Machine Gun Coy Relief of company was completed by 4.0 PM without incurring any casualties. On relief Sections marched back independently to	WA
AUSTRALIA CAMP N.22.B.28.			AUSTRALIA CAMP where they had tea and rested	WA

Confidential   Army Form C. 2118.

WAR DIARY of Artillery Machine Gun Corps.
INTELLIGENCE SUMMARY.
(Erase heading not required.) Ref Sheets 19. 40 S.W.

Instructions regarding War Diaries and Intelligence Summaries are contained in F. S. Regs., Part II. and the Staff Manual respectively. Title pages will be prepared in manuscript.

Place	Date	Hour	Summary of Events and Information	Remarks and references to Appendices
AUSTRIA CAMP COXYDE (N.23.B.3)	Oct 8 1917	9AM	At 9AM the Company embussed at Coxyde and moved off en route for Dunkerque arriving there about 11AM. The transport left Coxyde and proceeded by road, arriving in Dunkerque at 3.45PM. Weather rather boisterous.	W.A.
COUDEKERQUE BRANCHE	Oct 9 1917		Company in Billets resting. The day was devoted to cleaning up	W.A.
H.Q.A. 90.00	Oct 10 1917		Company attended Jay Funeral at 5PM. Weather rather cold and windy	W.A.
COUDEKERQUE BRANCHE	Oct 11 1917		Company in Billets training. Weather good. Casualties nil	W.A.
H.Q.A. 90.00. Oct 11 1917.				
COUDEKERQUE BRANCHE	Oct 11 1917		Company training in Billets training. Weather bet. Casualties nil.	W.A.
H.Q.A. 90.00. Oct 11 1917				
COUDEKERQUE BRANCHE	Oct 12 1917		Company in Billets training. Weather wet. Casualties nil.	W.A.
H.Q.A. 90.00. Oct 12 1917.				
COUDEKERQUE BRANCHE	Oct 13 1917		Company in Billets training. Weather wet. Casualties nil.	W.A.
H.Q.A. 90.00. Oct 13 1917.				
COUDEKERQUE BRANCHE	Oct 14 1917		Company attended Services under the various denominations. Casualties nil. Weather fair	W.A.
H.Q.A. 90.00. Oct 14 1917.				

WAR DIARY or INTELLIGENCE SUMMARY

Army Form C. 2118.

(Erase heading not required.) 4th Coy Motor Machine Gun Corps. Ref. Sheet 10. 1/40000

Place	Date	Hour	Summary of Events and Information	Remarks and references to Appendices
COUDEKERQUE BRANCHE H.11.A.90.60	Oct 15th 1917	4.15 AM	At 4.15 AM the company paraded and marched to DUNKERQUE where it embarked for GHYVELDE. At that place the company detrained and on completion returned to billets by barge route, arriving home at 1.5 PM. Weather bright.	WH
COUDEKERQUE BRANCHE H.11.A.90.60	Oct 16th 1917		Company in billets training. At 1.7 Noon the company paraded and marched to G.G.C.A.I. where it witnessed a Gas Demonstration given by Divisional Gas N.C.Os. The company returned to billets at 4.25 PM. Weather wet and windy.	WH
COUDEKERQUE BRANCHE H.11.A.90.60	Oct 17th 1917		Company in billets training. Casualties nil. Weather bad. Company attacked by Sounds. In the evening a Boche plane flew over DUNKERQUE and another towards COUDEKERQUE BRANCHE. Later it flew over COUDEKERQUE BRANCHE but no bombs were dropped.	WH
COUDEKERQUE BRANCHE H.11.A.90.60	Oct 18th 1917		Company in billets training. "B" Section at 12 noon paraded for an attack in co-operation with the 1st Highland Light Infantry. This practice attack was finished by 3 PM and the Section arrived back by 4.30 PM. The company fired a very good course in the evening.	WH

Confidential

Army Form C. 2118.

WAR DIARY of 4th Coy Machine Gun Corps

INTELLIGENCE SUMMARY.

(Erase heading not required.) Ref Sheet 19. 40.6.0.0

Instructions regarding War Diaries and Intelligence Summaries are contained in F.S. Regs., Part II. and the Staff Manual respectively. Title pages will be prepared in manuscript.

Place	Date	Hour	Summary of Events and Information	Remarks and references to Appendices
COUDEKERQUE BRANCHE	Oct 19/17		Company in billets training. Casualties nil. Weather bright.	W.A.
H.M.A.Gs.00.	Oct 19/17			
COUDEKERQUE BRANCHE	Oct 20/17		Company in billets training. Casualties nil. Weather good.	W.A.
H.M.A.Gs.00.	Oct 20/17		Company carried out firing practices on range at B.7.19.	
COUDEKERQUE BRANCHE	Oct 21/17		Company in billets training. Casualties nil. Weather good.	W.A.
H.M.A.Gs.00.	Oct 21/17		Lt J.S. Hamilton joined company from Machine Gun Corps Base Depot.	
COUDEKERQUE BRANCHE	Oct 22nd/17		Company in billets training. Casualties nil. Weather bright.	W.A.
H.M.A.Gs.00.	Oct 22/17			
COUDEKERQUE BRANCHE	Oct 23rd/17		Company in billets training. Casualties nil. Weather nil.	W.A.
H.M.A.Gs.00.	Oct 23/17			
COUDEKERQUE BRANCHE	Oct 24/17		Company in billets training. Casualties nil. Weather fair.	W.A.
H.M.A.Gs.00.	Oct 24/17		Coy was stood in readiness for the morels new area.	
COUDEKERQUE BRANCHE	Oct 25th/17		Company on removal at 8 a.m. and moved off en route for ERINGHEM.	W.A.
H.M.A.Gs.00.			Arrived at 1.30 P.M. Billets very scattered. Light draught horse died at 5 P.M. from stoppage. Weather very windy.	

WAR DIARY or INTELLIGENCE SUMMARY

Army Form C. 2118.

(14th Coy Machine Gun Corps)

Sheet 21 of 00
Ref Sheet HAZEBROUCK SHEET 5 1st 200

Place	Date	Hour	Summary of Events and Information	Remarks and references to Appendices
ETRINGHEM T.22.D.8.4.	Oct 26th 1917		Coy boarded at 9.45 A.M. and moved off at 10.15 A.M. for ARNEKE arriving there by 12 NOON. Weather very hot. Casualties nil. Billets very scattered	WA
LEDRINGHEM ARNEKE. C.27.C.9.8.	Oct 27th 1917		Company in billets training. Casualties nil. Weather fine.	WA
LEDRINGHEM C.27.C.9.8.	Oct 28th 1917		Company in billets training. Weather fair. Casualties nil. Commanding Officers of the Brigade visited the front area. These Commanders returned to 58th Division and stayed the night, returning next day. Company attached battalions under the various Commanders.	WA
LEDRINGHEM C.27.C.9.8.	Oct 29th 1917		Company in billets training. Weather good. Casualties nil.	WA
LEDRINGHEM	Oct 30th 1917		Company in billets training. Weather wet. Casualties nil.	WA
LEDRINGHEM	Oct 31st 1917		Company in billets training. Weather fine. Casualties nil.	WA

W Harrison Capt
O.C. 14 Coy M.G.C.

WAR DIARY of Finsbury Machine Gun Company

INTELLIGENCE SUMMARY

(Erase heading not required.)

Army Form C. 2118.

Vol 22

Place	Date	Hour	Summary of Events and Information	Remarks and references to Appendices
Bus	3rd Nov 17		Company in billets training. Routine for casualties.	
Bus	4th Nov 17		Company in billets in training. At 8.15 am letters moved off to co-operate with Battalions in a Brigade Tactical Exercise. The Company returned to billets at 1.0 pm	
Bus	5th Nov 17		At 8.15 am Company moved off to co-operate with Battalions in a Brigade Tactical Exercise. Company also did Section Training.	
Bus	6th Nov 17		Company in billets training. At 8.30 am the Company moved off to ANNEKE where it billeted. In the afternoon a few Lewis guns of the Company met the 90th Field Ambulance in a Divisional Football Cup 1st Round, and were defeated. Result 3 goals to nil.	
Bus	7th Nov 17		Company in billets training. Lewis gun team took part in Hickey Cup Competition Tie	

Confidential

WAR DIARY or INTELLIGENCE SUMMARY

Army Form C. 2118.

(Erase heading not required.)

Place	Date	Hour	Summary of Events and Information	Remarks and references to Appendices
[illegible]	[illegible]		Company in billets training. No casualties nil. Weather good	
[illegible]			Company in billets training. Casualties nil. Weather good	
[illegible]			Company being in billets training. Casualties nil. Weather good	
[illegible]			Company paraded at 9.10am to cooperate in a Brigade tactical scheme. Weather was a trifle wet. Casualties nil.	
[illegible]			Company in billets training. No casualties. Weather wet.	
OUDEZEELE			Company paraded at 11.45am and marched to billets in 15 Kmt. Company arrived in new area N.W. of OUDEZEELE at 2.30 pm	

WAR DIARY
INTELLIGENCE SUMMARY.
(Erase heading not required.)

Army Form C. 2118.

Place	Date	Hour	Summary of Events and Information	Remarks and references to Appendices
			Company marched to [illegible] at	
			arriving there by 12 noon. The weather was fine but road was	
			very muddy. The Company was accommodated in TUNNELLING	
			Coys	
	13th		Working in camp. Weather fine. Casualties nil	
			Company in camp. Weather fine. Casualties nil	
	14th		Company to camp. Weather fine. Casualties nil. Company	
			attended for Divine Service	
	15th		Company in camp training. Weather fine. Casualties nil	
	16th		Company in camp training. Weather fine. Casualties nil	
	17th		Company in camp training. Weather fine. Casualties nil	

Army Form C. 2118.

WAR DIARY of 2nd Montgomery [illegible] ~~INTELLIGENCE SUMMARY.~~
(Erase heading not required.)

Place	Date	Hour	Summary of Events and Information	Remarks and references to Appendices
F.24.C.	18th Nov 17		Company in camp. Company attended lectures & also under the various Commanders.	
F.24.C.	19th Nov 17		Company in camp training & 9.30 am att. Officers went down to BOESINGHE N.G.O.R.I. visited the Canal bank. Neither side shelling. Weather mild.	
F.24.C.	20th Nov 17		Company in camp training. Transport station and in training by the Commanding Officer. Weather good.	
F.24.C.	21st Nov 17		Company in billets training. Officers visited Ypres & POPERINGHE and viewed in raising map of M.E. Corps front. Neither side shelling much.	
F.24.C.	22nd Nov 17		Commanding Officer (Lt Col [illegible]) with [illegible] Lieuts visited front line trenches and [illegible]	

Confidential

WAR DIARY
or
INTELLIGENCE SUMMARY.
(Erase heading not required.)

Army Form C. 2118.

Instructions regarding War Diaries and Intelligence Summaries are contained in F.S. Regs., Part II. and the Staff Manual respectively. Title pages will be prepared in manuscript.

Place	Date	Hour	Summary of Events and Information	Remarks and references to Appendices
F.M.C.	Nov 27/17		Guns in gun camp having Ord. with new D.Q.M.H. North (2.6) with new	
H.G.R.15.			Billeting parties at BRIELEN (H.6.A) Hutton and Lieut Moss at	
			3rd/Divisional Commander Ammunition Column/Brigade in British Camp	
			W. F. 21.B.	
Staff to	Nov 27/17		Munshot N.H. H. at 8am and proceeded by march route to	
Camp at			REIGERSBURG CAMP (H.6.9.58) arriving there at 12.30 pm.	
Guns Sheet			Company paraded at 2.15 pm and marched to POPERINGHE STATION	
H.6.A.5.B.			where it entrained to BRIELEN. The detrainment was successfully	
B27/2 6.5.			effected at 5.30 pm. Company then marched to camp at	
Wanstect			B.27/2 6.5. arriving there at 6.30 pm.	
H.Q.R5.	Nov 28		Company in billets training. At 7.30 hrs. 6 gun teams parading	
Wanstect			and proceeded to the line and were temporarily attached to 94th	
			Infantry Brigade. Distribution as follows. 4 teams occupying a	
H.G.R.B.B			Pill Box at D.5.B.H.3 and 2 teams occupying a Pill Box at	
			D.1/D.8.8. Casualties Nil. Weather good.	

Confidential

WAR DIARY of Anthsley Machine Gun Corps. Army Form C. 2118.

INTELLIGENCE SUMMARY

(Erase heading not required.) Sheet 28 N.W. 1/40,000.

Instructions regarding War Diaries and Intelligence Summaries are contained in F. S. Regs., Part II. and the Staff Manual respectively. Title pages will be prepared in manuscript.

Place	Date	Hour	Summary of Events and Information	Remarks and references to Appendices
Ad Qrs. B.27.A.6.5. Transport B.30.D.1.2.	26th Nov 17		Nos. remaining teams of "C" Section bivouced at 7pm and bivouced to the line at D.4.P.88. One team under Lt. I. Rothwell and the team under Lt. E. G. Salles. A working party of 40 ORs was found by company which proceeded to the line, and was employed for carrying ammunition, to the various gun positions. This party was moved by Motor Lorries or journeys to and from camp. 1 OR wounded	[signature]
Ad. Qrs. B.27.A.6.5. Transport B.30.D.1.2.	27th Nov 17		"B" and "D" Sections relieved "A" and "C" Sections in the line. Sections relieving were under the command of Lt. L.O. Fairbairn and Lt. N. Shannock respectively. Weather inclement. No casualties	[signature]
Ad Qrs. B.27.A.6.5. Transport B.30.D.1.2.	28th Nov 17		A working party was found for carrying ammunition etc. to the various gun positions. 2 ORs wounded. Weather good.	[signature]

Confidential

WAR DIARY of 141st Coy Machine Gun Corps
INTELLIGENCE SUMMARY

Army Form C. 2118.

(Erase heading not required.) Ref Sheet 28 NW. 1/10,000.

Place	Date	Hour	Summary of Events and Information	Remarks and references to Appendices
In Res B.27.A.6.5. Transport B.30.D.1.2.	29th Nov 17		Company in camp resting. C.O. visited the line and chose Barrage positions for 16 guns, in vicinity of D.5.C.4.5. Casualties Nil. Weather Fair.	
In Res. B.27.A.6.5. Transport B.30.D.1.2.	29th Nov 17		At 2pm, a working party paraded and proceeded to the vicinity of D.5.C.4.5. where it made indirect fire positions and carried ammunition. Remainder of company — less transport — marched off at 7pm to IRISH FARM CAMP at C.27.A.00.60. Limbers was effected without incident. Casualties nil. Weather good.	
In Res. B.27.A.6.5. Transport B.30.D.1.2.	30th Nov 17		At 2pm remainder of Company moved up into the line in preparation for the forthcoming operations. Casualties 1 O.R. killed in action. Weather cold.	

Confidential

WAR DIARY Further Machine Gun Corps. Army Form C. 2118.
INTELLIGENCE SUMMARY.

(Erase heading not required.) No. that 70 Belgium Mo. 208

Instructions regarding War Diaries and Intelligence
Summaries are contained in F. S. Regs., Part II.
and the Staff Manual respectively. Title pages
will be prepared in manuscript.

Place	Date	Hour	Summary of Events and Information	Remarks and references to Appendices
HD QRS AT				
D.H.C. DE POPERINGHE	1st to 4th Feb 1918		Company in the line. Pretty quiet	
	5th Feb 1918		Company in the line with Brigade to give in forward zone by intense	attached
	10 Feb 18		Out of the line. 10 days in Poston in case of German advance L.of C.	
			Spent the time of duty in the line interim of nothing sort happened	OR

Army Form C. 2118.

WAR DIARY
or
INTELLIGENCE SUMMARY.

(Erase heading not required.) 17th (N.Midland) Divisional Machine Gun Corps. No. 20 1/1/20,000

Instructions regarding War Diaries and Intelligence Summaries are contained in F. S. Regs., Part II. and the Staff Manual respectively. Title pages will be prepared in manuscript.

Place	Date	Hour	Summary of Events and Information	Remarks and references to Appendices
HD QRS at				
TRANSPORT AT H.Q. 4. 3	Sep 1st 1917		Company in billets training. Weather fair. Casualties nil	
HD QRS at TRANSPORT AT H.Q. 4. 3	Sep 2nd 1917		Company in billets training. Weather fair. Casualties nil	WA
HD QRS AT H.3.B.4.3	Sep 3rd 1917		Company in billets training. Weather fair. Casualties nil	WA
HD QRS AT H.3.B.4.3	Sep 4th 1917		Company in billets training. Weather fair. Casualties nil	WA
TRANSPORT H.3.B.4.3	Sep 5th 1917		Lieut J.T. Dunn joined Company from Base Depot. Company in billets training. Weather fair. Casualties nil	WA
HD QRS AT H.3.B.4.3	Sep 6th 1917		Lieut G.A. Kott joined Company from 219th Company on appointment to second in command. Weather fair. Casualties nil	WA
HD QRS AT	Sep 16th 1917		Company in billets training. Weather fair. Casualties nil	WA
TRANSPORT H.3.B.4.3	Sep 17th 1917		Company in billets training. Weather fair. Casualties nil	WA
HD QRS AT TRANSPORT H.3.B.4.3				

WAR DIARY

Euthley Machine Gun Corps. Army Form C. 2118.

INTELLIGENCE SUMMARY.

At Sheet 28.Belgium 1/40,000

Place	Date	Hour	Summary of Events and Information	Remarks and references to Appendices
HD QRS CANAL BANK	Dec 18th 1917		Company less Transport and Quartermasters Stores moved up to CANAL BANK EAST in support of 96th Machine Gun Coy. Casualties nil. Weather good.	
TRANSPORT A.T. H.3.B.4.3.				WA
HD QRS CANAL BANK	Dec 19th 1917		Company in billets training. Weather good. Casualties nil.	WA
TRANSPORT H.3.B.4.3				
HD QRS CANAL BANK TRANSPORT H.3.B.4.3.	Dec 20th 1917		Company in billets training. Weather fair. Casualties nil.	WA
HD QRS CANAL BANK	Dec 21st 1917		2 teams of "A" Section moved up at 0.30 am under 2/Lieut A.L. WILDER to proceed to the line to relieve 2 teams of "A" Section in the line. Weather fair. Casualties nil.	WA
TRANSPORT H.3.B.4.3			Company in billets training.	
HD QRS CANAL BANK	Dec 22nd 1917		Company in billets. Weather good. Casualties nil.	WA
TRANSPORT H.3.B.4.3.				
HD QRS CANAL BANK	Dec 23rd 1917		Company in billets preparing to go to line. Weather good. Casualties nil.	WA
TRANSPORT H.3.B.4.3				

WAR DIARY or INTELLIGENCE SUMMARY.

Army Form C. 2118.

(Erase heading not required.) Ref: Nov. 28 Column 3/11/1918

Place	Date	Hour	Summary of Events and Information	Remarks and references to Appendices
HD QRS. C.IK.D.	16.35 Nov 27 1917		Company moved up into the line. Weather fair. Casualties nil.	WA
TRANSPORT H.3.B.4.3				
HD QRS C.IK.D.	16.35 Nov 28 1917		Company in line. Weather very cold. Casualties nil.	WA
TRANSPORT H.3.B.4.3				
HD QRS C.IK.D.	15.35 Nov 26 1917		Company in line. Weather extremely cold. 4 casualties nil.	WA
TRANSPORT H.3.B.4.3				
HD QRS C.IK.D.	15.35 Nov 29 1917		Company in line. Weather good. Casualties nil. 1 O.R. joined Coy.	WA
TRANSPORT M.B.B.4.3				from Base Depot.	
HD QRS AT C.IK.D.	15.35 Nov 28 1917		Company in line. Weather extremely cold. 1 O.R. killed.	WA
TRANSPORT H.3.B.4.3				
HD QRS C.IK.D.	15.35 Dec 2 1917		Company in the line. Weather very cold. D.R. wounded.	WA
HD QRS C.IK.D.	15.35 Dec 3 1917		Company in the line. Weather very cold. Casualties nil.	WA
HD QRS C.IK.D.	15.35 Dec 3 1917		Coy was relieved by 117th M.G. Coy. on night of 31/1st Dec 1918. Relief was completed by 3 am. Coy withdrew from line to IRISHFARM.	WA

W. Harrison Capt.
O.C. 116 Coy. M.G.C.

14TH COMPANY MACHINE GUN CORPS.

REPORT on the Action of the 14th Company Machine Gun Corps during recent Operations, 1st to 3rd Dec, 1917.

The Company under my command were called upon in co-operation with 188th Company forming a group (of which I was in Command) to put down a Barrage, and to carry out harassing fire on a given point in the enemy's lines, during Operations 1st to 3rd December, in conjunction with groups of Machine Guns on the Right and Left.

All the necessary orders were issued and I took my Battery Commanders on to the ground and taped out the Battery Positions as soon as possible after receiving my orders.

I experienced great difficulty in obtaining suitable ground for Battery Positions owing to the following reasons: -

(a). The ground alloted to my group was very badly cut up by shell-fire and in places water-logged.

(b). More than 75% of my area was almost continually under shell-fire.

(c). Movement by day was very restricted.

The time given to make emplacements, belt filling Shelters and cover for the men was not sufficient, consequently I decided to pay the most attention to the making of the emplacements.

Each gun had to have with it: -
    24,000 rounds S.A.A.
    20 Filled Belts.
    3 Petrol Tins.
    Oil.
    Rations for 48 hours for all ranks.

The question of getting this material up to the gun positions presented great difficulty.

Owing to the shortage of personnel of the 188th Company my Company was called upon to assist them in their preparations which meant an extra strain on my men.

I however impressed on all ranks that all 32 guns had to be in position ready to fire by 5.p.m. on "Y" day. Upon being told this all ranks put their shoulders to the wheel and worked splendidly consequently, all 32 guns (No. 1. Group) were laid on their Barrage Lines by 5.p.m. ready to open fire on "Y" day.

At Zero plus 8 minutes, all guns opened fire in accordance with 32nd Division Instructions No 7, Appendix "A".

After carrying out the first phase of the Operation it was found necessary to amend Appendix "A".

This was done in accordance with instructions received.

No. 1. Group was not called upon to concentrate.

During the Operations I had the following casualties: -

    2 Officers................Killed.
    9. O.Rs. .... "
    14. O.Rs. ....Wounded.

P.T.O.

I do not consider the casualties large, taking into consideration the amount of time spent in preparing the positions, carrying ammunition to gun positions, and the number of rounds of S.A.A. fired.   I estimate the number of rounds fired by my Company during the Operations at 300,000 rounds (three hundred thousand) and by No. 1. Group at approximately 550,000 rounds (five hundred and fifty thousand) rounds.   During the Operations I had 2 guns and 2 Tripods completely destroyed.
I had also one or two minor casualties to guns, tripods, etc, all of which can easily be repaired and made fit for use again.

APPENDIX "A" ISSUED WITH 32nd DIVISION OFFENSIVE INSTRUCTION No. 7. (MACHINE GUNS).

Battery.	Times.	Task.
A.B.C.& D.	(a) Zero plus 8 minutes to Zero plus 2 hours. (b) 6.a.m. to 8.a.m. (c) 3.30p.m. to 5.30p.m. (d) On S.O.S. Signal.	(a), (b), (c);- Open fire on S.O.S. line. One gun of each sub-section will remain on this line, the other will search continuously between the S.O.S. line ans extreme range, paying particular attention to the vicinity of dug-outs, occupied shell-holes, tracks, etc. (d) Fire on S.O.S. line.

Rate of Fire etc.

(a) During the three Barrage periods 50 rounds per gun per minute.

(b) On S.O.S. Signal- 1 belt in first minute, then 100 rounds per minute for 10 minutes then 60 rounds per minute till situation clears.

(c) Harrassing fire.
Occasional bursts of will be fired during the day of attack and following night on selected targets in areas alloted to Batteries.

Confidential

WAR DIARY
or
INTELLIGENCE SUMMARY

Army Form C. 2118.

of 14th Coy Machine Gun Corps

BELGIUM 1/100,000
Reference Sheet HAZEBROUCK 5A

WO 95/24

Place	Date	Hour	Summary of Events and Information	Remarks and references to Appendices
Coy HQ Ors BERTHAM.	Jan 1st 1918		At 4-30 AM Company moved from Irish Farm and marched to Siding at BOUNDARY ROAD where it entrained en route for POPERINGHE. At 9-30 AM the Company entrained at POPERINGHE and moved off for AUDRUICQ arriving there about 3-30 PM. Motor Trucks were then taken to BERTHAM where Company was billeted. Weather very cold. Casualties 2 ORs Killed 3 ORs Wounded.	WA
Coy HQ Ors BERTHAM.	Jan 2nd 1918		Company in billets Resting. Weather cold and snowy. Casualties NIL	WA
Coy HQ Ors BERTHAM.	Jan 3rd 1918		Company in billets training. Weather very cold. Casualties NIL	WA
Coy HQ Ors	Jan 4th 1918		Company in billets training. Weather very cold. Casualties NIL 2/Lieut E.T.J. Tapp. Joined Coy from Base Depot.	WA

Confidential

WAR DIARY of 9th Coy Machine Gun Corps Army Form C. 2118.
~~INTELLIGENCE SUMMARY.~~   BE.GWM. 100,000.
(Erase heading not required.)   Reference Sheet HAZEBROUCK 5 A.

Instructions regarding War Diaries and Intelligence Summaries are contained in F. S. Regs., Part II. and the Staff Manual respectively. Title pages will be prepared in manuscript.

Place	Date	Hour	Summary of Events and Information	Remarks and references to Appendices
Coy HdQrs BERTHAM	Jan 5th 1917		Company in Lewis training. 10 O.R.s joined Company from Machine Gun Base Depot. Weather very cold. Casualties NIL	WA
Coy HdQrs BERTHAM	Jan 6th 1917		Company in Lewis training. Weather extremely cold. Casualties NIL	WA
Coy HdQrs BERTHAM	Jan 7th 1917		Company was inspected by the 19th Infantry Brigade. 13 inspected. Weather very cold. Casualties NIL	WA
Coy HdQrs BERTHAM	Jan 8th 1917		Company in Lewis training. Weather very cold. Casualties NIL	WA
Coy HdQrs BERTHAM	Jan 9th 1917		Company in Lewis training. Weather extremely cold. Casualties NIL	WA

Confidential

WAR DIARY
of
14th Coy Machine Gun Coy Army Form C. 2118.
INTELLIGENCE SUMMARY.

BELGIUM. 100,000.
Reference sheet *HAZEBROUCK 5A

(Erase heading not required.)

Instructions regarding War Diaries and Intelligence
Summaries are contained in F. S. Regs., Part II.
and the Staff Manual respectively. Title pages
will be prepared in manuscript.

Place	Date	Hour	Summary of Events and Information	Remarks and references to Appendices
Coy Ho Qrs BERTHAM	Jan 10th 1917		Company in billets Training. Weather very cold. Casualties NIL	WA
Coy Hd Qrs BERTHAM	Jan 11th 1917		Company in billets Training. Weather extremely cold. Casualties NIL	WA
Coy Ho Qrs BERTHAM	Jan 12th 1917		Company in billets Training. Weather very cold. Casualties NIL	WA
Coy Ho Qrs BERTHAM	Jan 13th 1917		Company in billets Training. Weather Extremely cold. Casualties NIL	WA
Coy Ho Qrs BERTHAM	Jan 14th 1917		Company in billets Training. Weather snowy & cold. Casualties NIL	WA

Confidential

WAR DIARY
or
INTELLIGENCE SUMMARY.
(Erase heading not required.)

Army Form C. 2118.

$\frac{1}{14}$th Coy Machine Gun Corps

BELGIAN $\frac{100,000}{}$

Reference Sheet HAZEBROUCK 5A

Instructions regarding War Diaries and Intelligence Summaries are contained in F. S. Regs., Part II. and the Staff Manual respectively. Title pages will be prepared in manuscript.

Place	Date	Hour	Summary of Events and Information	Remarks and references to Appendices
Coy HQrs BERTHAM	Jan 15th 1917		Company in Billets Training. Weather Cold & snowy. Casualties NIL	WA
Coy HQrs BERTHAM	Jan 16th 1917		Company in Billets Training. Weather Very Fair. Casualties NIL	WA
Coy HQrs BERTHAM	Jan 17th 1917		Company in Billets Training. Weather Cold. Casualties NIL	WA
Coy HQrs BERTHAM	Jan 18th 1917		Company in Billets Training. Weather Cold. Casualties NIL	WA
Coy HQrs BERTHAM	Jan 19th 1917		Company in Billets Training. Weather Very Fair. Casualties NIL	WA

Confidential

WAR DIARY of 140th Coy Machine Gun Corps

INTELLIGENCE SUMMARY

Army Form C. 2118.

BELGIUM, FRANCE
Reference Map HAZEBROUCK 5A

Place	Date	Hour	Summary of Events and Information	Remarks and references to Appendices
Coy HQRS	Jan 20th 1917		Company in Billets Training. Transport preparing for the move to the new Area.	
BERTHAM			Weather very cold.	
			Casualties NIL	
Coy HQ	Jan 21st 1917		Company (less Transport) in Billets Training & preparing for the move to the new Area. Transport less (2 limbers & Water Cart) moved off in a three days trek by road to the new area. Starting point was passed at 8-32 a.m. Starting Point, Cross Roads just North of the Y in NORBASQUES (Hazebrouck 5A Map) First days trek was as follows:- NORBASQUES - MOULLE - SERQUES - ST MOMBLIN - BROXELLE	
BERTHAM			Weather very fair	
			Casualties NIL	

Confidential

WAR DIARY
or
INTELLIGENCE SUMMARY
(Erase heading not required.)

Army Form C. 2118.

9/14th Coy. Machine Gun Corps. BELGIUM + FRANCE

Reference Sheet 28. 1/40.000.

Place	Date	Hour	Summary of Events and Information	Remarks and references to Appendices
Coy. H.Q.Rs Bigd 33.	Jan 22nd 1917		Company (less Transport) moved off from BERTHAM, at 6.45am, by march route to RODTVIC8, and arrived at 8.0AM. The Company entrained at 11.0am for VLAMERTINGHE, and detrained at 2.30 PM, arrived in camp at HOSPITAL FARM at 5.30 PM. Transport by march route. Received days pack passed through ERKELSBRUGGE - ZEGGARS CAPPEL - ESQUELBECQ - WORMHOUDT and billeted in the village of HOUTKERQUE. Weather fair. Casualties NIL.	WH
Coy. H.Q.Rs Bigd 33.	Jan 23rd 1917		Company (less Transport) in Billets observing Kitts, Equipment etc., Transport arrived in camp at Hospital Farm at 2.30 PM. Weather very cold. Casualties NIL	WH

1/12th Coy Machine Gun Corps Army Form C. 2118.
BELGIUM + FRANCE

WAR DIARY
or
INTELLIGENCE SUMMARY.
(Erase heading not required.)

Reference Sheet 28 1/40,000.

Place	Date	Hour	Summary of Events and Information	Remarks and references to Appendices
Coy H.Q Qrs B.19.D.33.	Jan 24th 1918		Company in Billets Training. Casualties Nil. Weather Very cold. 9 ORs joined company from the 219th Machine Gun Company	W.A
Coy H.Q Qrs B.19.D.33.	Jan 25th 1918		Company in Billets Training. Casualties Nil. Weather Fair.	W.A
Coy H.Q Qrs B.19.D.33.	Jan 26th 1918		Company in Billets Training. Casualties Nil. Weather very cold.	W.A
Coy H.Q Qrs B.19.D.33	Jan 27th 1918		Company in Billets Training. Casualties Nil. Weather extremely cold.	W.A
Coy H.Q Qrs B.19.D.33.	Jan 28th 1917		Company in Billets Training. Casualties Nil. Weather very cold.	W.A

WAR DIARY
INTELLIGENCE SUMMARY

of 14th Coy Machine Gun Corps
BELGIUM & FRANCE
Army Form C. 2118.

Reference Sheet 28th 1/40,000

Place	Date	Hour	Summary of Events and Information	Remarks and references to Appendices
Coy HQRS B.19.d.33	Jan 29th 1918		Company in Billets Training. Weather very good. Casualties Nil.	WA
Coy HQRS AMBROSE CAMP B.10.D	Jan 30th 1918		Company moved from HOSPITAL FARM (B.19.d.33.) to AMBROSE CAMP (B.10.D.) Transport moved from HOSPITAL FARM (B.19.d.33) to DEWEY CAMP (A.11.d.9.5.) Weather fair. Casualties Nil	WA
Coy HQRS AMBROSE CAMP B.10.D	Jan 31st 1918		Company in Billets Training. Weather fair. Casualties Nil	WA

W Hanvent Capt
O.C. 14 Coy M.G.C.

Confidential

WAR DIARY Fifth Machine Gun Corps
INTELLIGENCE SUMMARY.

Army Form C. 2118.

(Erase heading not required.)

Instructions regarding War Diaries and Intelligence Summaries are contained in F. S. Regs., Part II, and the Staff Manual respectively. Title pages will be prepared in manuscript.

Director,
Kemmel - Bluingluer 28 W. 1/20,000

Place	Date	Hour	Summary of Events and Information	Remarks and references to Appendices
H.Q. GRS V.21.c.2.1.	8/10/18		Company relieved the 96th Machine Gun Coy in the No 1 Brigade Sector.	
TRANSPORT F.14.B.5.6.			Returned, established by O.A.S. on casualties nil. Weather good.	A/A
H.Q. GRS V.21.c.2.5.1.	9/10/18		Company in the line. Casualties 1 O.R. Wounded. Weather good.	10/A
TRANSPORT F.14.B.5.6.				
H.Q. GRS Avr. B.55 V.21.c.2.1.	10/10/18		Company in the line. Casualties nil. Battalions of Brigade were relieved by 27th Infantry Brigade of the 35th Division.	40/A
H.Q. GRS DIKKEBUSCH	11/10/18	1415	Company was relieved by 104th Machine Gun Company & 35th Division on the completion of relief the company embused at 1030 pm.	
TRANSPORT				10/A
R.S.C.50.20			Weather good.	
H.Q. GRS DICKORT CAMP	12/10/18		Company in billets resting and cleaning up. Casualties nil.	
TRANSPORT R.S.C.27.20			Weather good.	10/A
H.Q. GRS DICKORT CAMP	13/10/18		Company in billets. Casualties nil. No fire drill.	
TRANSPORT R.S.C.27.20			Weather good.	10/A
H.Q. GRS DICKORT CAMP	14/10/18		Company in billets training. Weather good. Casualties nil.	
TRANSPORT R.S.C.27.20				10/A

WAR DIARY or INTELLIGENCE SUMMARY

Army Form C. 2118.

Confidential

1/4th Bn. Machine Gun Corps.

Vol 25

Place	Date	Hour	Summary of Events and Information	Remarks and references to Appendices
Hd. Qrs. B.J.C. 20.10. TRANSPORT	27 Feb. 1918		Companies in billets training. Casualties - Nil. Weather	W.A
A.E.C. 50.70.				W.A
Hd. Qrs. U. D. 10.30. TRANSPORT B.11.B.5.5.	2nd "		Companies moved up into the line and relieved the 9th M.G. Coy. The relief was carried out successfully and without incident. By 9.15 p.m. Casualties nil.	W.A
Hd. Qrs. U. D. 10.30. TRANSPORT	3rd " 1.10.18		Company in line. Weather good. Casualties nil.	W.A
Hd. Qrs. U. D. 10.30. TRANSPORT B.11.B.5.5.	4th & 5th 1918		Company in line. Weather good. Casualties nil.	W.A
Hd. Qrs. U. D. 10.30. TRANSPORT	6th & 7th 1918		Company in line. Weather good. Casualties nil.	W.A
Hd. Qrs. B.J.C. 20.40. TRANSPORT	8th Feb 1918		Company was relieved in the trenches last night by 9th M.G. Company. Relief was successfully completed by 7.30 p.m. after which the Company proceeded in Motor Lorries to AMBROSE and CONES.	W.A
Hd. Qrs. B.J.C. 20.40. TRANSPORT B.11.B.5.5.	9th Feb 1918		Company in billets resting. Weather good. No casualties.	W.A

Army Form C. 2118.

WAR DIARY
or
INTELLIGENCE SUMMARY.
(Erase heading not required.)

Place	Date	Hour	Summary of Events and Information	Remarks and references to Appendices
HD QRS				
DEPORT CAMP TRANSPORT A.S.C. 50.20	5 Feb/18		Company in Lillers training. Weather good. Casualties nil.	WA
HD QRS DEPORT CAMP TRANSPORT A.S.C. 50.20	6 Feb/18		Company in Lillers training. Weather good. Casualties nil.	WA
HD QRS DEPORT CAMP TRANSPORT A.S.C. 50.20	7 Feb/18		Company in Lillers training. Weather good. Casualties nil. 2/Lt J.G. Bread joined Company from Base Depot.	WA
HD QRS DEPORT CAMP TRANSPORT A.S.C. 60.20	8 Feb/18		Company in Lillers training. Casualties nil. Weather very good. Company attended a Demonstration in Gas at Lillers.	WA
HD QRS DEPORT CAMP TRANSPORT A.S.C. 50.30	9 Feb/18		Company in Lillers training and preparing to move to the line. Casualties nil. Weather good.	WA
HD QRS DEPORT CAMP TRANSPORT A.S.C. 50.20	10 Feb/18		Company moved and relieved the 91st M.B. Coy in the HET 595 Sector and relieved successfully completed. Casualties nil.	WA

Army Form C. 2118.

WAR DIARY of 251st Machine Gun Corps
or
INTELLIGENCE SUMMARY
(Erase heading not required.)

Instructions regarding War Diaries and Intelligence Summaries are contained in F. S. Regs., Part II. and the Staff Manual respectively. Title pages will be prepared in manuscript.

Place	Date	Hour	Summary of Events and Information	Remarks and references to Appendices
H.D. Q.RS U.G.R.20.60 TRANSPORT A.11.B.5.5.	1st Feb 18		Bombardment in the line. Casualties nil. Weather good.	WA
			R.H. Wings and Details moved to Goesinghe Camp (R.5.D.6.3)	
			Machine Gun Coys to be formed into Machine Gun Battalion	
H.D. Q.RS U.G.R.20.60 TRANSPORT A.11.B.5.5.	22nd Feb 18		Bombardment in line. Casualties nil. Weather good.	WA
H.D. Q.RS U.G.R.20.60 TRANSPORT A.11.B.5.5.	3rd Feb 18		Bombardment in the line. Casualties nil. Weather very good.	WA
TRANSPORT A.11.B.5.5. H.D. Q.RS U.G.R.20.60	4th Feb 18		Bombardment in the line. Casualties nil. Weather very good.	WA
H.D. Q.RS U.G.R.20.60 TRANSPORT A.11.B.5.5.	5th Feb 18		Bombardment in the line. Casualties nil. Weather very good.	WA
H.D. Q.RS U.G.R.20.60 TRANSPORT A.11.B.5.5.	7th Feb 18		Bombardment in the line. Casualties nil. Weather very good. Battalion moved back to Dekort Camp	WA
			Stores and Details of the Battalion	

Confidential

WAR DIARY of 187th Machine Gun Company
or
INTELLIGENCE SUMMARY.

Army Form C. 2118.

Bizschote 1/10/0
[illegible]

(Erase heading not required.)

Instructions regarding War Diaries and Intelligence Summaries are contained in F. S. Regs., Part II. and the Staff Manual respectively. Title pages will be prepared in manuscript.

Place	Date	Hour	Summary of Events and Information	Remarks and references to Appendices
HD QRS U.18.20.6	27 Feb 18		Company in the line. At 4.57 am the Company took up barrage whilst the 174th Infantry Brigade made a raid into the enemy's lines. This barrage was maintained till about 11.15am when normal conditions were resumed. 74,000 rounds of fire. No casualties.	N.A.
TRANSPORT H.11.B.59				
HD QRS U.9.A.3.6.	28 Feb 18		Company was relieved by the 97th Machine Gun Company. The relief was completed by 10 pm. Guns and teams were left in Corps Line Reserve under 2/Lt T.B. Gates. Casualties nil. Weather good.	N.A.

W. Cannand Capt.
O.C. 187 Coy. M.G.C.

www.ingramcontent.com/pod-product-compliance
Lightning Source LLC
Chambersburg PA
CBHW082010220426
43670CB00014B/2597